POSSUM LIVING

POSSUM LIVING

How to Live Well Without a Job and With (Almost) No Money

by Dolly Freed

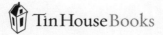

Tin House Books

Printing History:
Universe Books edition published October 1978
Three printings through October 1979
Bantam edition published April 1980
Tin House Books edition published January 2010

Published by Tin House Books, Portland, Oregon, and New York, New York
Distributed to the trade by Publishers Group West, 1700 Fourth St., Berkeley, CA 94710, www.pgw.com

Library of Congress Cataloging-in-Publication Data

Freed, Dolly.
 Possum living / by Dolly Freed.
   p. cm.
 ISBN 978-0-9820539-3-5
 1. Life skills—United States. 2. Unemployed—United States—Life skills guides. 3. Cost and standard of living—United States. 4. Housing, Rural—United States—Finance. I. Title.

 HQ2039.U6F7 2010
 646.70086'94—dc22
                              2009034057
Printed in Canada
Cover and interior design by Janet Parker

www.tinhouse.com

Contents

Foreword

Possum Living, by the pseudonymous Dolly Freed, was probably out of print by the time I stumbled across it in 1985, in the attic above the woodshed of a fixer-upper farmhouse I'd bought in Washington County, New York. The previous owners had been city people whom the house, as well as a death in the family, had defeated, and they'd left behind a pile of books that suggested all too clearly they'd cherished the same back-to-basics fantasies that had brought me there. Many of these volumes dealt with such specific and practical matters as building decks and preserving vegetables; *Possum Living* was a manifesto. True, it offered hands-on advice—recipes for such foraged vegetables as yellow rocket, tips on raising and butchering rabbits, a diagram of a woodstove made from an old oil drum—but more notably it made a new version of the centuries-old argument for quitting the "money economy" in favor of a freer way of life. ("Freed" chose her pseudonym cleverly.) The book's grocery-bag brown cover and its typewriter-style typeface, complete with ragged-right margins, suited the post-hippie, reduced-expectations gestalt evoked by its subtitle: *How to Live Well Without a Job and With* [the word *Almost* careted in, in faux handwriting] *No Money*.

My parents had also fetishized—and to a great extent achieved—a life of rural simplicity, and when I was growing up, their generation's equivalents of *Possum Living* still sat on their bookshelves: such Depression-conditioned survivalist tracts as Maurice Grenville Kains's 1935 *Five Acres and Independence* and Louise Rich's 1942 *We Took to the Woods*. Freed published her book in 1978, the middle of the Carter era, with a small outfit called Universe Books; the following year, Bantam reprinted it as a mass-market paperback. They must have thought it would appeal to the outdoorsy, countercultural, basically nostalgic readers who, a few years back, had bought the *Whole Earth Catalog*, the Foxfire books, and Euell Gibbons's *Stalking the Wild Asparagus*. But Dolly Freed makes clear from the get-go that she's no high-minded advocate of the American pastoral: "Why is it that people assume one must be a hippie, or live in some dreary wilderness, or be a folksy, hard-working, back-to-nature soybean-and-yogurt freak in order to largely by-pass the money economy?" she writes in her introduction. "My father and I have a house on a half-acre lot 40 miles north of Philadelphia, Pa. (hardly a pioneer homestead), maintain a middle-class façade, and live well without a job or a regular income—and without working hard, either." Freed presents herself not as a utopian, but as a subversive survivor in a corrupted world, without ideological illusions. "We live this way for a very simple reason: *It's easier to learn to do without some of the things that money can buy than to earn the money to buy them* . . . . So if you're thinking spiritual or sociological thoughts, don't waste your time with me." For her totem animal, Freed fixes on the ignoble possum— "the stupidest of animals," but "fat and sassy" and able to survive "almost anywhere, even in big cities." Rather than embrace such sentimental icons as the soaring eagle, or even the lone wolf, she identifies herself with a varmint.

Freed frames *Possum Living* as a call to change your life— "It's feasible," she writes in her peroration. "It's easy. It *can* be done. It *should* be done. Do it"—but her contempt for any form of idealism makes it hard to believe that she cares much what society at large does, as long as it leaves her alone. And despite her repeated claims that you can be "lazy" and survive on $700 a year (even in 1978 dollars), the possum life seems arduous enough: gardening, canning, fishing, hunting and raising animals for meat, foraging, cooking, gathering wood for the stove—not to mention making the stove. And fixing up the fixer-upper. Freed and her father bought their suburban house for $6,100, but the plumbing was ruined, the brick walls were crumbling, the cellar floor was mud, the wiring was faulty, and the windows were broken. Their do-it-yourself repairs, she reports, took less than a year, but it must have been a hell of a siege. All this primal work was surely less alienating than the factory labor her father resolved never to endure again, but it can't have been the Edenic existence that Shakespeare's Gonzalo fantasizes about in *The*

Tempest: "No occupation; all men idle, all; / All things in common nature should produce / Without sweat or endeavor; . . . but nature should bring forth, / Of its own kind, all foison, all abundance, / To feed my innocent people."

Whatever Freed or her publishers thought *Possum Living* was, I see it as both a classic of American cantankerousness—like Thoreau's *Walden*, Melville's *Moby-Dick*, Frost's "Build Soil," or Pound's *ABC of Economics*—and a cryptic autobiography. Freed was supposedly eighteen when she wrote this book—and I see no reason to doubt her—and here and there she gives glimpses of a rancorous, downwardly mobile, borderline-violent milieu, something like the world of her contemporary Raymond Carver. "A friend of ours," she notes in passing, in a chapter on "everyday nitty-gritty law," "lost his cool and threatened his wife's lawyer in open court." Freed's own parents were divorced, and her father, whom she calls the Old Fool, also had trouble with his wife's lawyer: "So Daddy visited his house that night and caught his attention." How? Freed doesn't say, but her recommendations for dealing with an "adversary" include making anonymous threatening phone calls late at night, followed up by a visit to his house, during which you "do something to let him know he has an enemy who has no intention of playing the game by his rules"—cutting his phone line, for instance, or throwing a brick through a window, or slashing his tires, or poisoning his dog. The gentle ecopuritan readers of Euell Gibbons and the *Whole Earth Catalog*—assuming they ever got this far into *Possum Living*—must have realized that Dolly and the Old Fool weren't their sort of people.

It's not hard to get a fix on the Old Fool: Freed calls him "a working stiff," who "sometimes . . . made good money and felt like a big shot," and at other times "was out of work and scared." He seems to have been an autodidactic crank. "I remember when I was a little girl Daddy painted a picture of Diogenes sitting in his barrel tossing away his drinking cup. He wrote 'Are you a Diogian?' as a caption and hung it on the living room wall to inspire us. Mom wasn't inspired." But Dolly's still in the process of forming a self. At one moment, she's a tough-talking right-wing libertarian: "Americans of my social stratum don't put much stock in government and law. I don't think I know an adult man who doesn't own a gun—'just in case.'" The next moment, she's the coy all-American girl: "Then there's BOYS!—but enough of that." Out of nowhere, she inserts a poem with the self-deprecating title "Dolly's Autumn Doggerel": "Sun kisses cheek, breeze musses hair / Geese call to us from high in air . . . ." One of the great pleasures of *Possum Living* is to see her trying on her personas, and putting a hopeful face on what must often have been a difficult existence.

Possum Living actually did change my life, though in a way Dolly Freed could never have intended. It directly inspired parts of my first novel, *Jernigan*, which gave me my career as a fiction writer and, consequently, as a teacher. Like Dolly and the Old Fool, my protagonist's girlfriend is a suburban survivalist who raises rabbits in her basement; the .22 pistol she uses to kill them becomes a crucial prop in the story. If I hadn't happened on *Possum Living, Jernigan* wouldn't have been the same novel;

there might not even have *been* a novel. I cite her book in my acknowledgments, but I've never heard from Dolly—whoever she may be. (That was in 1991, and both my dog and my phone line are still okay.) I owe her one, and I hope that in introducing her to a new generation of readers I can give back some of what she's given me.

—David Gates

Introduction

Many people, perhaps you among them, are not temperamentally suited for the 9-to-5 rat race but assume there is no other way to live. Too proud to accept charity (welfare, food stamps) and not at all interested in joining a hippie commune, or pioneering in the boondocks, or wheeling and dealing in business, or crime—what else is there? Others are unemployed and worried sick over that. Are these thoughts and fears grounded in fact?

Why is it that people assume one must be a hippie, or live in some dreary wilderness, or be a folksy, hard-working, back-to-nature soybean-and-yogurt freak in order to largely by-pass the money economy? My father and I have a house on a half-acre lot 40 miles north of Philadelphia, Pa. (hardly a Pioneer homestead), maintain a middle-class facade, and live well without a job or a regular income—and without working hard, either. (Of course, the term "live well" is open to various interpretations. We think we do—others may disagree.)

One main ingredient in our well-being is being able to hear

the financial news without supposing the end of the world is at hand. The leading economic indicators, the balance of payments, the energy crisis, inflation, unemployment, the GNP—what are they to us? Each evening on the six o'clock news the economists, the natural heirs of the medieval scholastic theologians, trot out all their nonsense and solemnly present it as being of cosmic significance. Now, why is this? After all, mankind was living on Earth-and often living well—for thousands of years before the dogma of "growth" and the rest of our present economic catechism were invented.

My father and I produce most of our food and all of our drink (and fine food and drink they are, too, if I do say so myself) and spend only about $700 each per year. And as I said, we imagine we live well. While not overly religious, we do heed the Biblical admonition that "every man should eat and drink, and enjoy the good of all his labour, it is the gift of God" (Ecclesiastes 3:13).

Notice it says "God," not "GNP."

We aren't magic. Neither of us does anything any other reasonably able person can't do—you, for instance.

In this book you will find much practical information for saving money, but telling you *how* to do so isn't my only goal. Frankly, I hope to inspire you to do some independent thinking about economics as it affects the course of your individual life now and in the coming "age of shortages."

1.
We Quit the Rat Race

Do you remember the story of Diogenes, the ancient Athenian crackpot? He was the one who gave away all his possessions because "People don't own possessions, their possessions own them." He had a drinking cup, but when he saw a child scoop up water by hand, he threw the cup away. To beat the housing crunch he set up an abandoned wine barrel in a public park and lived in that.

The central theme of Diogenes' philosophy was that "The gods gave man an easy life, but man has complicated it by itching for luxuries."

Apparently he lived up to his principles. But despite that handicap he seems to have had the most interesting social life imaginable. He not only lived in the center of the "Big Apple" of his day (5th century B.C. Athens), he also had the esteem and company of many of the most respected, rich and influential citizens, including that of the most expensive prostitute in town.

When Alexander of Macedon, the future conqueror of the known world, was traveling through Greece, he honored Diogenes with a visit.

Alexander admired Diogenes' ideas to the point of offering him any gift within his means. Diogenes, who was working on his tan at the time, asked as his gift that Alexander move aside a bit so as to stop shading him from the sun. This to the richest and most powerful man in the Western world.

Parting, Alexander remarked, "If I were not Alexander, I would be Diogenes." Diogenes went back to nodding in the sunshine.

Diogenes was fair and just to all but refused to recognize the validity of man-made laws. He was a good old boy, one of the first back-to-basics freaks in recorded history. He lived to be over 90. Alexander, The Mighty Conqueror, drank himself to death at age 33.

Well, this "Saint Diogenes" has been my father's idol for many years. I remember when I was a little girl Daddy painted a picture of Diogenes sitting in his barrel tossing away his drinking cup. He wrote "Are You a Diogian?" as a caption and hung it on the living room wall to inspire us.

Mom wasn't inspired.

At the time, Daddy was a working stiff of the ordinary garden variety. Sometimes he made good money and felt like a big shot. Other times he was out of work and scared. Our well-being was at the mercy of fluctuations of the economy in those days, same as it is for millions of other people.

Why should this be? What did Diogenes do, besides live in a barrel, that anyone can't do today? The economy of his society wasn't as prosperous as ours, yet he didn't work and he didn't starve.

It happens that something of a Diogian life is still possible, because Daddy and I are now living it. Here's what happened:

After Daddy painted the picture of Diogenes, we initiated austerity measures. Daddy hoped we could get some money in the bank and become more secure and independent.

Mom's hobby, candlemaking, came in for some scrutiny. We had candles from one end of the house to the other, and the equipment and supplies were beginning to be a financial drain. Rather than give up candlemaking, Mom decided to sell her candles to recoup the money she had spent.

To our complete surprise, she started making really good money at it. In less than three months she was netting more than Daddy was bringing home from the factory. We couldn't believe it! Unsuspected by all of us, including Mom herself, she turned out to have a flair for craftspersonship and an absolute genius for salespersonship. It was a women's lib fantasy come true—a mother and housewife suddenly discovering she had the ability to make money on her own. In short order Mom rented a store and opened a regular business. Daddy quit his job at the factory to help run it. Being good with numbers and miserly, he took over the bookkeeping and financial chores. Having no previous experience or knowledge of the principles of business or economics, the two of them just bumbled along, not knowing what they were doing, and evolved their methods using ordinary common sense.

They made a bundle. Moreover, they cooked the living bejeezus out of the books and so managed to keep most of it. But we weren't happy, so after three years we sold the business and our home and moved out to this more rural area. The plan was to have a small shop in our home—just enough to pay the bills—and to relax and enjoy life for a change.

Alas, it wasn't to be. Mom and Daddy started arguing all the time. About money, of course. When they didn't have any, they didn't argue about it—when they did, they did. Mom, having gotten a taste for money and wheeling-and-dealing, found she didn't want to give it up. No Diogian she. So she took little Carl, my brother, and left. Soon thereafter, she obtained a divorce.

Well, that was four years ago. When the dust had all settled from the divorce, Daddy and I found we had no car, no TV, no appliances, no job, no job prospects, and no income. Without Mom we couldn't run the candle business, and Daddy is flat not going back to factory work.

What we did have left was this house, free and clear, and a little money in the bank.

For us emotional types, a divorce can be a very trying experience. Making decisions about one's future is difficult for some time following. So we haven't made any. The Old Fool likes to go around saying he can't decide what he wants to be when he grows up. But truthfully, not *having* to make decisions is one of the great luxuries of life—right up there with not having to go to work.

We just drift along from day to day. We have a roof over our heads, clothes to wear, and we eat and drink well. We have and get the good things of life so easily it seems silly to go to some boring, meaningless, frustrating job to get the money to buy them, yet almost everyone does. "Earning their way in life," they call it. "Slavery," I call it.

Sometimes Daddy frets and says we are little better than possums living this way. Possums can live most anywhere, even in big cities. They're the stupidest of animals, but there were possums on Earth millions of years before men appeared, and here they are—still going strong. Who can say if we or they will outlast the others in our good green world? They're all fat and sassy and love life (or so I like to believe), and nothing you can do will persuade one to work in a factory or office. Possum living is what we call our life here now.

So we live like possums? Good! Let us do so even more.

2.
The Cost Of Living

What do you think it cost to live in this country in 1976? According to the Department of HEW, or the Department of Agriculture, or another one of those damn-fool agencies—I forget which—it costs $5,500 per year to have a family of four maintain a "Normal Standard of Civilized Decency" or some such nonsense as that. (I have the facts somewhere on a newspaper clipping, but I can't find it.) If that's true, I guess my family of two, which spent about one-fourth of that, is by implication half-civilized—probably we're somewhere between neolithic savages and dibble-stick agricultural barbarians.

We have a neighbor who gets $30,000 and seems to feel his whole life has been ruined because he let his father talk him out of a job that paid $35,000. The job was a five-year contract in the Sahara Desert—or something like that, I believe.

Probably the ones he envies—the ones getting $35,000—can't stand it that Jones, who isn't half the man they are, is getting $40,000—an income that would enable them to live properly. Probably Jones likewise feels cheated. Keeping up with the Joneses doesn't work because the minute you pass the old Jones, a new one appears on the horizon. So why bother?

Let's get down to simplistic, logical reasoning. You wouldn't want Howard Hughes's money if you had to live Howard Hughes's life, right? And you wouldn't want to live a pure possum life either, right? Ergo, *ipso facto*, there exists a niche of financial ambition somewhere between those two extremes that is just right for you. It's up to you to decide where your niche lies.

For your consideration, however, let me try to influence you by our example to look more closely at the possum end of the possum/Hughes scale. About one rung up from the bottom you'll find Daddy and me. Between 1 August 1975 and 1 August 1976, we spent $1,498.75. When I totaled up the figures and handed them to Daddy, his face went all white. Then he sat down and checked that his heart was still working okay.

"Impossible!" he shouted. "Where did it all go?"

So nothing else would do—I must break it down to an itemized account. Here's where it all went:

Food $268.89
Moonshine ingredients 98.37
Soap and paper products 47.45

21

Fuel oil 161.66

Cooking gas 87.01

Electricity 101.24

Home improvement material (concrete,

    paint, etc.) 335.43

Property taxes 286.00

Clothing 13.33

Luxuries 25.05

Other (tools, laundry, fish hooks, etc.) 74.32

                                              $1,498.75

Then to get him calmed down, I pointed out that the item "Home improvement material" was nonrecurring, and since the stuff was used to increase the value of the property, it's like money in the bank. Take off that item and the budget reads $1,163.32.

Well, he muttered and sputtered awhile (out of habit), but he left smiling. Even a possum can make $1,163.32 per year, let alone two possums.

Having told what we *do* spend money on, let me now say what we *don't* spend it on.

In a word, hardly anything we can do without. Some people seem to be actively seeking ways to dissipate their money, and get nervous and upset if they fail to get rid of it all on a given shopping spree. It's burning that proverbial hole in their pocket. I've noticed this "drunken sailor syndrome" in all sorts of people, and I'm sure you have, too. I completely fail to understand it. Even folks on a back-to-basics trip will do it under pretext of necessity. Are $250 chain saws, $450 Franklin stoves, $90 food driers, and $1,200 snowmobiles "basics"?

We like the anecdote about the stranger in a small Vermont village. Walking down the street, he notices that the man walking ahead of him is provoking some peculiar behavior. The men glare at him or shake their fists. The women turn up their noses. The children are bustled across the street to avoid coming near him.

"What's going on?" he asks one of the villagers. "Is he a wifebeater? A drugpusher? A childmolester?"

"Nup. Dipped into his capital."

My kind of people! I think I could make a pretty good case for miserism, same as for my religious or political opinions, but I'm not going to do so. You either have that good old Silas Marner, Hefty Green, Jack Benny instinct, or you don't. All the rhetoric in the world won't change you, I know.

However, I would like to discuss thrift. If you are one of those who "just can't save," do a little arithmetic: Take your annual income, after taxes, and subtract the $6K needed to keep you civilized. Now multiply by, say, 5. Is it a pretty figure? Are the toys and trash—the "gracious living"—you would buy in the next five years really worth that?

Here are a few things we don't spend money on:
   * Insurance gets never a penny. Once when Mom and Daddy were still married, an acquaintance went into the insurance business and tried to sell

them life insurance.

"If I should die," said Daddy, looking Mom in the face, "money would mean nothing to her." That was probably the first time in the history of the world an insurance salesman didn't have a word to say.

We don't have fire insurance because we have a brick house, a fire extinguisher, a hose long enough to reach all parts of the house, a lightning rod, sound electrical wiring, neither of us smokes, and we're never away from home for long periods of time. We don't need flood insurance since we live on a hill, and we also don't need theft insurance (our movable possessions total less than $200 in value). We just see no reason for liability insurance. Not having a car saves us all the insurance associated with that.

* Vacations, another common expenditure, are not required—our whole life is just one big vacation. We don't need to "get away from it all" because there's nothing we want to get away from.

* Hobbies don't cost us much. Mine, birdwatching, requires a pair of binoculars and a book for identifying them, but they both last for many years. We both have $17 running shoes, but they last pretty long. We bought a badminton set for $11 (listed under "Luxuries"), but that, too, should give us years of enjoyment.

* Christmas doesn't exist for us. December 25 is just another day here. 'Tis the season to be greedy,

ostentatious, treacly sentimental, frenzied, hysterical, morbidly drunk and suicidal, and we see no reason to pretend otherwise. So we ignore it in the hope that it'll go away. Christmas has become like a horse with a broken leg. You can't enjoy the horse and simply ignore its broken leg—the only decent thing to do is put it out of its misery and be done with it. If you're religious, you surely realize that the potlatch orgy of December 25 has little to do with Christ. Mammon or Bacchus, maybe, but not Christ. So do yourself and your religion both a favor and refuse to play the game. If we *all* ignore it, it really *will* go away.

* Income tax wasn't listed on the budget, as you may have noticed. We don't pay any, because we never have enough income to require paying. Do you realize what a luxury that is? The rotten swindlers in Washington aren't lining their pockets with *my* money. *I'm* not paying the welfare chiselers to breed like flies. The idiotic federal giveaway programs don't cost *me* anything. You can't *imagine* what a difference it makes blood-pressure-wise if one is a taxpayer or not while one is reading the news!

We pay property taxes, because we have to (they really will sell you out if you don't), but we simply ignore the various municipal taxes. When the man came around about the "occupant headtax," we simply told him we didn't live here—we're just here fixing up the

25

place as a rental. He never came back. About two years ago we got a form in the mail about an "occupation tax," but since we don't have an occupation, we figured it didn't concern us.

* Being true misers, we find we can do without all sorts of little nonessentials that do add up: haircuts, "grooming aids," pets, "knickknacks" and other decorations, snacks and convenience foods, furniture, beauty parlor visits (I don't need them), magazines and newspapers (we use the library), telephone service, movies, toothpaste (we make our own—equal parts of salt and baking soda dissolved in water), tobacco, charity, gifts (a quart of wine or moonshine or a dressed rabbit does for gift giving)—but you get the picture. We keep a record of every cent we spend, so we do know just where it goes. Let me urge you to do the same: you'll be surprised at all the things that take your money— which means your time and energy. If you're buying anything on time, you want to find out what the actual interest rate and service charges are, of course.

"But don't you want Nice Things?" people ask. "Don't you like to go out and have a Good Time?"

"Nope," we answer. "Get a lot out of staying home reading."

"Oh yeah? What do you read that's so interesting?"

"Our bankbook."

3.
Income

It's really ridiculously easy to pick up the little bit of money we spend each year. I do babysitting for a working mother, and housework for an elderly couple sometimes. These people are neighbors, so it's no hassle. A friend of ours has a craft shop and I make up packaged items for her on a piece-rate basis every now and then. I pick up the materials, then do the work here at home.

We pick up a buck or two selling bunnies and herb plants. We just put up a sign on the front lawn when we have extra to sell.

Daddy does yardwork and handyman jobs for the neighbors occasionally, and even goes so far as to take on a regular job for a week or two at a time when the spirit moves him.

When we lived near Philadelphia and the candle business was slow, as it is in the summer, Daddy used to work for Manpower, the temporary help people. They pay coolie wages, of course, but you go to different jobs all the time and meet people, so it's very interesting. You don't stay on any one job long enough to become bored with it, and if you happen to dislike a particular job, you can turn it down without their holding it against you.

Much as I hate to admit it, you can really earn good money by making candles in your kitchen and selling them. Daddy and I would rather mug old ladies in the park for money than sell candles, but that's only because of our overdose experience. There's no reason *you* couldn't do it. If you're interested, go to any craft or specialty store and tell them what you want to do. Since they'll want to sell you the equipment and supplies, they'll be most helpful and cooperative. If you do try it, I hope you have enough sense to regard it as a business venture and don't get hung up on it as a hobby. Unfortunately, if you don't happen to have a sales personality you won't do well with candles or any other craft item. Trite, but true, though, quality candles practically sell themselves, and it's not really hard to make a candle of higher quality than the ordinary factory-made item.

Consignment placing in gift shops doesn't pay. The shopkeeper wants to big a bite, and also isn't going to push your item when he has a store full of things he has money tied up in. Fleamarkets are also bummers. You pay for your spot, then nickel-and-dime it all day. Partnership arrangements whereby one party produces and his or her friend sells *never* work unless both partners eat at the same table. Otherwise there are bound to be difficulties, and you're more likely to lose a friend than to make money. Most craft items such as ceramics or leather goods don't sell as well as candles or tasteful, well-made jewelry. I don't know why, but that's the way it seems, and we have a lot of experience in this field. However, if you have an unusual craft and can get some publicity on it, a fad might develop with you sitting right on top of the situation. Mom got her start by simply calling up the women's page editor of the local newspaper and saying she had a feature article for them. She got a half-page interview complete with photos out of it, free. It would have cost a good $200 to buy that advertisement.

Here are two good ways to sell craft items:

* If someone who eats at your table goes to school or works in an office or factory, they periodically take in samples and show them around. Orders taken must be promptly filled with quality merchandise or there won't be repeat business.

* Find a gregarious type to act as hostess and hold a "party" or "demonstration." She invites 12 to 25 friends over for a display and demonstration of your craft. (It had better be good.) Then you take orders. Afterward there's coffee or drinks and snacks or a buffet. The hostess gets $15 plus 10% of the gross (in merchandise) for her troubles, and $5 for every party booked at her party. (These things breed like rabbits.)

The question of sales tax might come up. Don't collect it if you aren't going to pay it! You might just be quiet about it. If some busybody brings it up, say you have applied for a tax number but haven't received it yet and can't collect tax till you do. If pressed on the matter, play dumb. (We were always good at that.) Or you can get a number and collect the tax, but that increases the price to your customers and complicates your life. Some unscrupulous folks rake off 30% or 40% from the state's share for their trouble.

Don't suppose that because, people live in nice neighborhoods and act graciously, they won't dead-beat on you, because they sometimes will. Explain to the hostess, *before* the party, that she is to collect the money and that it must be paid in full before the merchandise is delivered. Be polite but firm.

It shouldn't cost you more than about $20 to get started. Then you want to shop around for your supplies—there's a wide disparity in prices in this market.

Pricing your merchandise shouldn't be difficult. Keep track of your expenses and your time for making and selling the stuff, and you should be able to calculate it okay. You know what your time is worth to you. You might also note prices of comparable items for sale in local stores. Being handmade, your item might be of higher quality than the store item, and if it is, you shouldn't be shy about charging a bit more.

There are so many ways to pick up money without actually (shudder) 9-to-5-ing, that whole books have been written on just that subject. Check your library. There are also periodicals devoted to the subject, but these are mostly vehicles for people hawking various franchise deals, some of pretty dubious worth. Use your common sense and instincts to evaluate them.

But enough. Rather than make a lot of money, which sets you up as a John for the various taxing agencies and other predators, learn instead to do without much money. Make your own way, without buying what you need. Do it for yourself, instead. You become free that way.

4.
We Rassle with Our Consciences

Let me re-emphasize that we aren't living this way for ideological reasons, as people sometimes suppose. We aren't a couple of Thoreaus mooning about on Walden Pond here. (Incidentally, the reason Thoreau quit Walden Pond was that he was lonely— I don't care what he said. You need the support of a loved one.) No, if some Wishing Fairy were to come along and offer to play Alexander to my Diogenes, I'd pretty quickly strain that Wishing Fairy's financial reserves. We live this way for a very simple reason: *It's easier to learn to do without some of the things that money can buy than to earn the money to buy them.*

There actually are people living somewhat similarly for ideological reasons, though. In fact, there's a growing cult of this sort of thing going on, as you may know. Unfortunately, many of these people tie in all sorts of outlandish religious, mystic, and/ or nutritional theories with their possum living and give us all a reputation for weirdness. Many back-to-basics types also buy expensive and unnecessary equipment, clothing, and health-nut food (and wind up back in the money economy because of it) and so give us all a reputation for phoniness.

So if you're thinking spiritual or sociological thoughts, don't waste your time with me, but if you just want to easy-up your life somewhat, why, then, you're talking my language! We'll get that Protestant Work Ethic monkey off your back!

We're incredibly lazy. You wouldn't believe it! We have an anarchy here wherein neither has to do anything we don't feet like doing. (Except to feed the creatures. You can't neglect animals in your care.) Normally I do the housework and the Old Fool does the garden, the heavy work, and the care of the creatures. Not because we have sexist roles, but because the housework bugs him more than it bugs me, and vice versa. If I don't feel like doing the dishes, say, for a couple of days, why I just don't do them. I often feed the animals if Daddy feels like goofing off, and he often does the dishes. The anarchy works for us because we love each other and don't abuse it. It amazes me that so many people must either dominate or be dominated, like a bunch of monkeys on Monkey Island at the zoo.

Often my conscience tries to nag me when I'm goofing off,

but it doesn't get very far any more. Daddy says it's just the same with him. Actually, it's hard to understand how it is that laziness has fallen into such disrepute in our society. Well, I'm tired of being a Closet Sluggard! I'm lazy and proud of it!

We can afford to be lazy because we satisfy our material needs with little effort and little money. Of course, you know that money doesn't buy only goods and services, it also buys prestige and status. Being somewhat egocentric, we don't feel the need to buy prestige or status. The neat trick that Diogenes pulled was to turn the tables on those of his contemporaries who believed that "Life is a game and money is how you keep score." He didn't keep score. We don't keep score. You needn't keep score either if you don't want to. It's entirely up to you.

Money per se isn't the only status thing involved. Some people make a big machismo deal out of employment itself. You know, mighty-hunter-bring-home-the-bacon stuff. Folks old enough to remember the depression of the 1930s tend to take a very solemn attitude about jobs, and unless you like to argue, it pays to sidestep the issue with them. It doesn't matter that you're not on welfare or accepting charity but are earning your own way in life (albeit in an unorthodox manner), the mystique lies with that Holding Down a Job concept. Don't ask me why.

Sometimes people who secretly resent it that they have to work (or think they do), and we don't, point out that Daddy has no security for his old age. Daddy always knuckles under and mutters something like, "Gee, you're right, mutter, mutter," because it makes them feel better and doesn't cost him anything, so why not?

34

Once he was fishing and an old gentleman came along and struck up a conversation. Coming to the conclusion that Daddy couldn't find work, he started commiserating with him about the "hard times." Then Daddy made a mistake and let it out that he didn't *want* a job. The old boy got himself into a state of righteous indignation because he was retired, and had *earned* the right to go fishing on weekdays, by fifty years of hard work, and here Daddy was just going ahead *doing* it. Daddy mollified him by pointing out that he'd be up shit creek when he got old, and that thought cheered the old gentleman up to the point of giving Daddy a nice catfish he had caught.

However, what he truthfully thinks is:

* Sure, you have security, but the slaves on the plantation didn't starve either.

* The social security system is an obvious pyramid game and can't be trusted.

* There's really nothing I do now as a young man to live that I won't be able to do as an old man.

* It's unmanly to worry so about the future. Did Caesar worry about his old age pension when he crossed the Rubicon?

* Jesus clearly and specifically taught against concern for future security (Matthew 6:25–34). Like it or not, it's un-Christian to plan for the future.

* I refuse to spend the first sixty years of my life worrying about the last twenty.

* Dolly will take care of me.

These same resentful people might also bring up that "you aren't doing your share—you aren't contributing to society." While it's impossible to have too much contempt for this beehive mentality, to avoid an argument you can answer:

* I am too being useful! You can always use me as a
Bad Example!

* While I'm not contributing to economic growth, a
dubious good, I'm also not contributing to pollution, a
definite evil.

A serious consideration is that of family. I definitely plan to have children, although I'm not sure if I want to get married or not. I don't know many people who have been married for any length of time and are happy about it. I suspect the description of the average marriage—"Two animals find each other"—may be correct. Daddy says when I find the man I want to be the father of my children I can just invite him to move in. Why get the State of Pennsylvania involved? It's none of their business. If he doesn't want to move in, that's okay, too—he can visit. By the mores of our society I should leave here and go live with him, of course, but I don't see any reason why I should. I like the life I have here. Then, too, I don't want to leave the Old Fool alone as he approaches the downhill side of life. Don't suppose I'm sacrificing my happiness to my filial duty, because it's not that at all—I'm happier than most married women of my acquaintance, at least. Also, I want my children to grow up with their grandfather. The idea of the extended family—the generations living together—appeals to me. The notion of kicking the kids out of the old nest and sticking the old folks into some "retirement village" is part and parcel of industrialized economics, which I also dislike on other grounds. Possum economics allows for everybody to be useful and contribute to the well-being of the family, regardless of age. Young and old alike can, say, feed rabbits or run a still. The idea of genetic immortality—the family going on and on forever—appeals to me. It's the closest thing I have to a religion.

I'm trying to be fair with you and give you the picture of possum living as it really is. The few things I've mentioned that others may fault you on are no big deal—most people have enough to do to run their own lives without concerning themselves with what you are doing with yours. The big deal may be what you say to yourself. The Metaphysician-in-Residence—the little tiny unauthorized voice we all carry around in our heads—is going to chip in its two cents worth too.

"You know you're going to die eventually and they're going to throw you in a hole in the ground and shovel dirt in on top, don't you? Is *that* all you want to accomplish in life? To become a lousy possum?" it will sneer at you. "Is that the purpose of life? No! You've got to Make It Big," etc.

Not being a guru, I'm not going to go poking about in any purpose-of-life quagmire swamps with you. But really, what purpose can you find in the life of any human, living or dead, rich or poor, drunk or sober, that you can't read into a possum's life?

37

Possum philosophy was actually formed over 2,000 years ago, and I needn't go into it further. A good example of it is in the Book of Ecclesiastes, in the Bible.

Now that you have the overall idea—is it for you? Possibly not. It depends on the instincts you were born with and your present family circumstances. For example, my Mom wants no part of "this squalor," as she puts it. Daddy and I are instinctive possums—we break out in hives in elegant surroundings. Also, you have to *trust* your instincts. "Philosophize with a hammer," as Nietzsche advocated, "testing idols to see if they ring true." Does the money economy ring true for you? Does possum living ring true? It isn't enough that you know a false idol when you see one; your family must agree with you. If your kid gets the shakes when the TV goes on the blink, forget it. If your spouse gives you the fish-eye look when you mention rabbits in the cellar, forget it. If the thought of quitting your job blows your mind, don't do it. If it makes you feel good, on the other hand, do it! Damn the torpedoes, full speed ahead!

Now that you know what a lazy, rotten, sinful thing I am, I'd like to pass on to you some of the ideas we've picked up to help you become just the same. Besides the facts and examples I'm going to give you from our experience, you can learn how to do most anything that needs doing by simply researching in your local library. There's a growing body of literature on back-to-basics subjects and you can get information to help you there, too. Unfortunately, the editors of some of these periodicals seem to be willing to print articles by people with considerably more enthusiasm than common sense, so expect a lot of chaff among the wheat.

If you can't go the whole route, at least go part way. If you can't become a nonconsumer, aim to be a mini-consumer. Okay?

5.
Meat

Daddy and I love to eat. We have fast metabolisms and can eat like absolute hogs, never gaining an ounce. Being made this way by Nature, we naturally have a great interest in food and an appreciation of good eating.

But there's more to it than that. One of my earliest memories from childhood is of carefully hiding away a fishing line and hook so that "In Case of Emergency" I wouldn't starve. When his memory is jogged, the Old Fool says that in his childhood, he copied recipes for making bread for the same reason (although where he thought he could get flour when he couldn't get bread I don't know), so, you see, this isn't a frivolous subject with us.

Our present diet consists of the following:

   * Meat from rabbits we raise in our cellar
   * Eggs from chickens in the cellar

* Fish and turtles caught in local water

* Meat from game creatures

* Vegetables from our garden

* Wild mushrooms, hickory nuts and walnuts, berries and wild fruits, and a few edible weeds we gather free

* Grain from the grain store or that which we glean

* Grocery store items. We spend about $5.50 per week for things like cooking oil and margarine that it isn't practical for just two people to produce (although we could if we had to).

* About Killing Meat—Presenting a Case *

When you've raised a bunny or a chicken, it's kind of hard to kill it. Many people say that's why they won't raise their own meat. But someone had to kill the animals you buy in the store. People who will buy meat but won't kill their own are being hypocritical, it seems to me. If you're not a vegetarian, kill your own meat— don't hire someone else to do it.

Our bunnies never know they're going to die, even the second before we slaughter them. An animal commercially slaughtered was probably waiting in line to be killed, and was well aware of what was happening. Daddy takes the bunny in a box somewhere the others can't see and shoots it in back of the head with a .22.

The only reason we raise rabbits is to eat them. They wouldn't have been born if we didn't want them for meat. Isn't it better to be born and die than never to be born all? (Awful lot of metaphysics in carnivorism, isn't there?)

When you buy meat in a store, you never know what kind of chemicals were pumped into it, nor do you know what the animal that produced it ate, or what kind of hormones it was given. We know the bunnies are healthy and we know what they were fed.

The last stand of people who won't kill their own meat is "But how can I kill Fuzzy Bunny?—he's our pet!" or "But he's so cute." Well, there's nothing fuzzier or cuter than the little lambs that are sold as lamb chops. I cried when Daddy killed my ducky, but when it was roasted and on the table I made sure to get my share. In truth, a bunny or a duck doesn't have a personality, being simply too stupid.

We have a friend who won't eat mutton or rabbit because sheep and bunnies are cute, but will eat beef or pork because cows and pigs aren't (although I've seen some mighty pretty cows). The logic of her argument completely escapes me.

If you have never eaten a young domestic rabbit that was raised mostly on greens and grain, as opposed to commercial feed, you are most definitely in for a treat. Meat from the grocery store can't match that flavor.

Raising your own meat also gives you a feeling of independence, of accomplishment and competence that is a reward in itself. It gives me a sense of warmth and security to sit down in the cellar with the bunnies all hopping about. Sometimes I'll catch one and feel its haunch to see how it's coming along and imagine how good it will be.

* Rabbits *

You can get pamphlets on the subject free at your feed and grain store, or ask your librarian what they have or can get. There's also a good booklet you can get by sending 75¢ to the Superintendent of Documents, U.S. Government Printing Office, Washington, D.C. 20402, and asking for *Commercial Rabbit Raising*, Agricultural Handbook #309. Take what you read with a grain of salt, because they're either oriented toward commercial production, not home meat breeders, or else they're hawking their feed.

We raise our meat supply in a 14-foot-by-17-foot cellar, and no, it doesn't stink. If you were to come into our house your nose would never tell you there are rabbits and chickens on the premises. We take close to 300 pounds of meat out of that cellar per year. A cellar that size could produce the same amount even if it were located in a big city. Why not? We formerly kept the bunnies outside, but then were always worrying about bad weather, dogs, the waterbowls freezing, and our having to go out in severe weather to feed them. It's much more convenient the way we do it now.

We have simple wood, screen (chicken wire), and 14-inch-mesh hardware-cloth cages for our one mature buck and three breeding does. The floor of the cage is made of hardware-cloth, of course, since it supports the bunnies and allows most of the waste to pass through. Allow 6 square feet of floor area for each cage. The rest of our bunnies run loose on the floor. We aren't sure what their vitamin D requirements are, so we have the cages arranged so that the sunlight coming in through the windows falls on the mommy rabbits and their babies.

We breed each doe four times per year. The gestation period is only 30 days. Each doe's cage has a wooden box with a hole cut in the top for nesting. Five days before she's due, we put a pile of straw in the cage. The doe will use it to start building a nest. It's really comical to watch: she'll frantically grub up a mouthful of straw and leap into the box with it, reappear moments later and do it again. It's the one time in her life a doe'll show determination. The nest will then be lined with fur the doe plucks from her breast. (Although if she can get at the daddy, she'll yank fur out of him to use, too.)

If the doe produces more babies than she can properly nurse (you're pushing your luck with ten), we remove the puniest looking and drown them. This isn't as cruel as it seems, since some of them would probably die anyhow if we didn't. Don't try mothering baby rabbits with doll baby bottles, etc.; it doesn't work. The other babies are left with their mother for eight weeks.

Rabbits are often sterile during September and October, so you want to plan for that. We breed them at seven months of age and keep a breeder for three years.

Incidentally, incest is nothing to a rabbit, so choose your breeders on the criterion of how rapidly they grow to slaughter size, not who is who's brother, father, granny, Uncle Fuzzy, etc. One family tree consideration you might be interested in is flavor. Some lines of rabbits taste better than others for some reason, though the difference is generally slight.

Our experience is that the New Zealand white breed is best

for home meat production. They aren't as large at maturity as some other breeds, but they get there faster. If you decide to go into meat production, get good stock to start with. One good buck and one good doe are all you need to breed up a good herd. We fiddled around with various breeds and mixed breeds for a number of years, getting mixed results before finally wising up.

We very seldom use commercial pellets for food. (If you do, get a whole bag at a feed and grain store. You'll get ripped off at a pet store.) Bunnies grow slightly faster on pellets or other high-protein food, but they aren't necessary. In 1976, pellets cost about $5.00 per 50-pound bag, which will produce meat for about 40 cents per pound of dressed-out meat if you feed the pellets exclusively. (That's from the time the doe is bred till the litter is up to slaughter size.)

We feed corn, windfall apples and pears, soybeans (one government publication has it that rabbits don't like whole soybeans, but our experience is otherwise), green or dry maple leaves, weeds and grass, and discarded fruit and vegetables found behind grocery stores. (They don't mind if you take them, but it is polite to ask, and that gives you chance to mention your rabbits, which can save you some embarrassment.) When feeding weeds, give them a good variety, but try to get in plenty of clover, alfalfa, flowering plants, and other high-protein stuff. If you can't get many greens, consider growing alfalfa or clover in your lawn. As a general rule, rabbits' instincts keep them from eating poisonous plants, but foxglove, pokeweed, and any exotic-looking ornamental shrubs should be avoided. In the winter we note what the wild rabbits are eating and gather that. We often give our rabbits branches and twigs of maple to chew on. This keeps them from chewing the wooden cellar steps, and the green under-bark and buds are a good source of vitamins during the winter months, when greens may be scarce. (I've seen rabbits leave pellets for maple buds.) We grow a few sugar beets in the garden for the bunnies' winter use. The bunnies thrive on this diet. Indeed, a friend of ours who works for a feed company was surprised to see our bunnies were so healthy on a noncommercial diet.

They need clean water at all times. We usually give them some ordinary table salt, too. We spoil our bunnies by feeding them just about all they will eat.

Rabbits are hardy, healthy animals as a rule. They can stand cold very well, but if they get wet and can't dry off quickly they may die of pneumonia. It's especially important that their feet stay dry. Avoid letting your bunnies run around on the ground where they might pick up roundworms or other parasites. Dogs and cats can pass worms on to rabbits, too, so keep them away from the feed. Dogs have been known to knock over or break into cages and kill rabbits, so keep this in mind when building your cages if they are to be kept outdoors. Ear mites are the only other health problem our rabbits have encountered in our eight-year experience. A very inexpensive lime-sulfur mixture (bought from the feed and grain store) is mixed with water and dabbed on the brown scaly skin of the ear every other day till it starts to disappear (about three applications will do).

Be careful about allowing small children around rabbits; they can easily injure one by mishandling. Never pick up a rabbit by its ears. Grasp the skin over its shoulders with one hand and support its ass end with the other arm. If it struggles, you might get a nasty scratch if you're not careful. Putting its head under your armpit so it can't see usually has a calming effect.

* Slaughtering Rabbits *

When you slaughter an animal, you owe it to the creature to kill it quickly and painlessly—but you knew that. Shoot it or break its skull with a heavy club. Don't fool around with other methods—a .22 bullet costs only 2¢. We slaughter the young bucks first because we don't want any unscheduled breeding. We slaughter them when they weigh 4 to 6 pounds. A 2-pound animal is scarcely worth the trouble, yet that's what some people recommend.

We feel it's our duty to eat as much of the animal as possible. We collect the blood and cut out the tongue before skinning. These go into sausage.

The sooner you skin a killed animal the easier the job. We do it on the kitchen table. Slit the skin on the underside of the hind legs from foot to foot. Leave the feet on till the end of the job to use as handles. Cut the skin around in a circle at the hocks (ankles), and work it off to the body. On a young doe it will just slip off—on an old buck you'll have to cut away at the connective tissue pretty often. Work the skin down to the tail, anus, and sex

47

organs, and cut these away. Then slip it off the body like peeling a rubber glove off your hand. When you get to the skull, cut off the head. If you do that before skinning, you usually get hair on the meat. We take out the brain to add to the sausage.

Next cut off the back feet and rinse the carcass. Pinch up some of the abdominal flesh and carefully start a slit in it. If you just go ahead and stick the knife in, you'll likely open an intestine, which makes an unnecessary mess. Enlarge this slit to ass and throat. Remove the heart, liver, and kidneys, with some of the fat around them, and set aside. Remove the gall bladder from the liver, being careful to keep the gall off the meat. If some does spill, wipe it off immediately. Discard the windpipe and add the lungs to the sausage meat. Also add the thyroid, adrenals, excess and internal fat, spleen, and testicles or uterus, to be ground up in the sausage. Pick up the carcass and dump the stomach and intestines into a bucket or something. Rinse off the carcass, and the job is done. It's really easier than it sounds. I was doing it when I was 10.

You will soon evolve your own recipes, so I'm not going to go into great detail on that subject. You can fry rabbit, bake it, boil it for soup, or treat it the same as any other meat. We like it best fried with leaves of tarragon inserted into slits cut in the meat. In the summer, we often barbecue it over a hickory fire. There is a certain weed, yellow rocket, that combines with it perfectly in a soup. The liver, heart, and kidneys are usually fried for breakfast or added to a sauce for spaghetti. Don't overcook the liver! In, quick brown, and out is the rule. You know the animal was healthy, so you needn't overcook the meat for health reasons. Many people don't like liver because they cook it till it's like shoe leather. They expect it's going to be icky and deliberately over-cook it, hoping to cook the ickiness out of it. However, the *less* you cook liver, the better it tastes.

RABBIT SAUSAGE

* Collect the blood when you slaughter the rabbit.
* Save the tongue, meat scraps, lungs (minus windpipe), brain, spleen, thyroid, adrenals, excess fat, internal fat, and testicles or uterus.
* Mix in herbs. Thyme, fresh, tender sage leaves, and shallots or onions give the sausage a Lebanon bologna sort of flavor. Fennel, tarragon, and chives give it a warm, subtle taste.
* Run through a fine meat grinder.
* Mix in the blood.
* Run some raw wheat through the grinder.
* Mix the wheat with the blood mixture until you have it stiff enough to form patties. (Sometimes we simply use flour for the filler, but then it's not as good.)
* Cook the patties in a double boiler about 10 minutes. They are dark, almost black, when done.

Occasionally we save a section of large intestine, wash it well, stuff the mixture into it, tie up the ends, cook it 15 minutes in slowly simmering water, then hang up to dry. Sometimes we dry it over a smoky hickory fire. It's absolutely delicious, but it's a lot of trouble for the amount you get.

* Chickens *

We have three hens in the cellar for eggs. A friend traded them to us for a dressed rabbit. Before that, we had one hen, but it refused to eat and soon died. We think it was lonely. We acquired a baby duck once and, remembering the chicken, gave it a mirror. He became very attached to his little friend.

Chickens are extremely easy to raise. In fact, if we didn't keep them for economic reasons, I might even be tempted to keep them as pets. They're friendlier than the bunnies, and let you pet them, and they make pleasant clucking sounds all day. They also do good by eating insects and by picking up grain spilled by the bunnies.

We feed them corn, cracked soybeans, unused fishing worms, crushed rabbit bones, fish innards, and crushed eggshells (from their own eggs), and they also pick around in the bunnies' greens. We often let them go out and scratch around in the yard. Eggs from hens on this sort of diet have a rich flavor much superior to the bland "egg factory" product. I had heard that before but assumed it was just another health-nut myth until we started getting cellar-produced eggs. Chickens need grit, but if you just let them out occasionally they'll find their own. Otherwise, just a handful of gravel of various small sizes will do. They should have water at all times, of course. Don't forget to provide them with a nest box with some straw in it.

We get about a dozen eggs per week, but better hens would lay about half again as many. The activities of hens' ovaries vary with the hours of light in the day and can be manipulated with artificial lights. There are free pamphlets at the feed store that explain it, but it's a rather complicated subject and the small-time home producer needn't worry about it.

* Pigs *

Rabbits do us fine for meat because there's just the two of us, but they would be too small for a much larger family. Pigs are pretty efficient animals to raise but get too big for most people to handle. I don't guess you could keep them in your cellar, as they stink so much more than rabbits. There's a type of pig that reaches a mature weight much lower than ordinary, and it seems to me they'd be ideal for home meat production. If you're interested, write to J. H. Belknap, PIGmeePIG Project, The Hormel Institute, 801 Sixteenth Avenue, N.E., Austin, Minnesota 55912, and ask for information.

* Goats *

Goats used to be kept for milk even in cities until zoning laws came about. We had a goat once, but it made so much noise we had to get rid of it. (We gave it to a black neighbor. Next day he was back complaining the goat was prejudiced—it had knocked his boy down. Daddy assured him it knocked down white boys, too, and then he was satisfied with it again.) I think goats make noise out of loneliness. With more than one, you might be okay. Friends of ours keep two nannies which supply enough milk for their family of five. Although they're easy to raise, we don't have any because we're not that fond of milk.

* Game Meat *

Hunting is in ill repute with many people, and I can sympathize with their point of view to some extent. We see plenty of the Red-Hatted Brigade stomping about here blasting anything that moves—little tiny doves and squirrels, with maybe two ounces of meet on them, or anything else. It's a wonder they don't lobby for a hummingbird season. And then, too, killing something just for sport or money is a disgrace.

The Eskimos, the most consummate race of hunters humanity has ever produced, have an entirely different approach to the subject. They have it that game creatures are to be treated with dignity and respect and killed only to satisfy their legitimate necessities. Amen to that.

Don't be too tender to shed a little blood. Your ancestors weren't, and you wouldn't even be here on this good planet if they were, so rap with them across the centuries—kill and eat some game.

Game is more plentiful than most people suppose. There's probably five hundred tons of it flying around in Philadelphia alone in the form of pigeon meat. That isn't an exaggeration.

Pigeons are consistently excellent eating, besides being more plentiful and less wary than other game. We've gotten them by all sorts of methods, they're so stupid.

We formerly had a trap made of chicken wire, with an entrance consisting of stiff wires that were hinged to swing in but not out. The pigeons walked into it and the wires kept them from walking back out. (Someone stole the trap, and we haven't gotten around to building a new one yet.) We baited it with cracked corn and wheat.

Then we used ordinary rat traps of the spring-loaded type, with a grain of corn tied to the pedal, or trigger, and other grain scattered about to draw the pigeons. If you leave the trap in plain view and don't disguise it, they may be suspicious of it for a few days, but then they'll get used to it and go for the bait.

Ordinary pump-air rifles or CO_2 rifles are efficient tools for getting pigeon meat. You don't have to own one yourself, for invariably some neighborhood kid will. Tell him you like pigeons, and he gets to gratify his killer instinct, guilt-free, and you get that good meat. Everyone's happy but the pigeons.

We haven't tried it ourselves, but I've read of people scattering liquor-soaked bread, and gathering up the pigeons when they get too drunk to fly. Often at night we planned to do this but then next morning we'd find there wasn't any liquor left.

People who raise pigeons as a hobby often simply destroy unsatisfactory birds (such as homing birds that take too long to come home). If you ask these people they might either give them to you or sell them for a nominal price. These birds are referred to as culls.

Pigeons supposedly harbor disease (psittacosis), but so what? Wash your hands after cleaning them and you'll have no problem. Daddy knew a man who slaughtered them commercially and handled literally thousands of pigeons without ever catching psittacosis or anything else from them. (Ironically, he was also president of the local Audubon Society for many years.)

One more thing: Although you could net them by hundreds in any big city park, don't do it. Many cities periodically spend thousands to solve the "pigeon problem," but if you try to help them out, the SPCA will have you arrested. I don't get it either.

You could try this. Wear white lab smocks and carry clipboards. Net up the pigeons and scribble away at the clipboards every so often. You'll probably get your haul without harassment.

We don't get as much game as we'd like because, frankly, Daddy and I are neither one of us good shots or endowed with an overabundance of patience to snare them. We appreciate and gratefully eat up any game meat that comes our way, and could almost certainly survive on game (in one form or another) if we had to, but it really is easier to keep bunnies and chickens in the cellar.

Most people (including us) have unreasonable food prejudices. Charles Darwin was perhaps one of the few exceptions. On his famous *Beagle* voyage, he hogged up a veritable Noah's Ark of exotic meat as part of his research—or was he a gourmet in biologist's clothing? Try to get over your food prejudices same as you do for other illogical thinking.

Following is a partial list of game creatures we happen to know something about. By "game" I mean animals not specifically raised or commercially exploited for meat. One other thing—if you get an old creature, or a particularly masculine male, it might not come up to your expectations. Don't be discouraged from trying that species again; you might have better luck next time.

Armadillo: Rather common in Florida. So stupid you can actually catch them by hand. Slowly move up behind one and grab it by the tail. Quickly get the back legs off the ground so it can't pull away. (Daddy says he averaged about 50% success grabbing at them.) Cook the same as any other meat, except that toward February the males get rank and must be boiled to be fit to eat. Their livers are excellent. When Mom was pregnant with Carl, armadillo liver was the one thing she craved.

Cat: The SPCA says we have an enormous stray cat problem in this country. In some parts of the world this situation would be viewed as an opportunity, not a problem. The one person I know who claims to have eaten cat said it tasted like rabbit.

Deer: We don't kill deer because it would be too much meat for just the two of us. We let our deer-hunting friends know we like organ meat (tongue, heart, liver), and if they don't care for this "variety meat" they often give it to us. Some people actually give the liver to the dog, which is the exact opposite of what primitive hunters do. They eat the liver and give the steak to the dog, more

55

often than not.

Dog: Another opportunity disguised as a problem. (See Cat.)

Dove: It's a shame to kill a dove for the little meat on it, but people do, so you might as well not let it go to waste. Frankly, the meat is gourmet fare.

Duck: The finest meat in all of my experience—providing the duck ate right: grain or clean aquatic plants. If that duck grubbed around in mud or caught fish for its living, it's going to be barely edible.

Frog: The legs taste like slightly fishy chicken.

Goose: Very common, very big, and very good.

Grasshopper: We caught a bunch in our back yard and ate them, fried, as an experiment. They tasted like crunchy fish milt.

Groundhog or Woodchuck: If you see a groundhog grazing away from its hole, you can sometimes get him by racing, not for the groundhog, but for the hole. He'll run straight to the hole, and if you get there first you can dispatch him with a club. Groundhog liver tastes exactly like lamb liver. The meat itself is best boiled for soup or stew.

Horse: For thousands of years mankind has eaten horse and still does in some parts of the world. There's no rational reason to eat a cow and not a horse. (Same goes for pony and donkey.)

Long pig: For emergency purposes only. Formerly, fanciers claimed that the European subspecies was unpleasantly salty, tough, and stringy—others much better. It's generally lacking in Vitamin B.

Mountain lion: According to Darwin, the exact flavor of veal. The gauchos that Darwin befriended lived almost entirely on meat, and could therefore be considered experts on the subject. They preferred mountain lion to all other meat. (Don't kill one, though—they're getting scarce.)

Muskrat: The meat of thousands of these unfortunate animals is wasted annually by the fur industry. Muskrat hams are esteemed in many parts of the country.

Pheasant: Young pheasant are good, but an old pheasant isn't much better than an old chicken. Pheasants are so common here we often find them freshly killed by cars and aren't so finicky as to waste that good meat. In the winter, if the temperature hasn't been above the freezing point for some time, we take home any traffic-killed game we find. We once came upon a weasel killing a pheasant and got a free meal out of that. Don't—I repeat, don't—let pheasants "hang," as some cookbooks recommend!

Possum: We don't eat Possum for totemic reasons, but those who do say they're good. There have been proposals for raising them as commercial meat.

Rabbit: Cottontails are good, but pretty small. We know nothing of other types of wild rabbits.

Raccoon: Much the same as possum. I suspect the flavor might vary widely according to the animal's diet.

Small birds: Starlings taste almost like doves. They're so small, they're not worth cleaning; just cut out the breast meat. I've read of people catching and eating robins that were drunk on fermented berries (the robins were drunk, not the people, although the people may have been, too, for all I know). Again, they're really too small to bother with.

Snake: Snake meat is sold commercially and eaten (I suspect for braggadocio purposes) by some people. Fish-eating snakes probably aren't much good. Others probably are.

Squirrel: Good if they've been eating nuts; bland, if acorns or grain. Too small to fool with, in any case.

Turtle: See below, page 76.

Wild pig: Common in some southern localities. A slightly tougher, slightly gamier version of the domestic item.

Woodchuck: See Groundhog.

Woodcock: After corn-fed scaup duck, the best meat I know. Unfortunately, not very common, and rather small. We bake them, undrawn, then chop fine the intestines and flambé them in double-distilled moonshine.

To end the subject, two notes:

Many wild creatures are adapting themselves to human overpopulation. I've seen wild deer inside the city limits of Philadelphia, for instance. In situations where creatures are struggling to survive, don't further harass them by preying on them, but do take game with a free conscience where they are plentiful.

Theoretically, fooling with wild animals may be a health hazard. A low-virulent strain of bubonic plague is harbored by some West Coast rodents, for example. Any mammal, including pets, might contract rabies. If the animal appears healthy, and you wash your hands after handling it, and cook it properly, you'll be perfectly safe.

6.
Fish

In some parts of the world people live mostly on fish. Daddy and I love fish, and when they are biting good we really put them away. We kept a sort of economy ledger once and found that in one three-week period we ate 75 sunfish, 5 bass, 1 crappy, 1 catfish and 1 sucker.

We have several small streams and a lake within easy walking distance. This water is posted "No Fishing" and patrolled, so Daddy wears his running shoes when he goes fishing. Possums don't have money to squander on licenses, exotic equipment, or store-bought bait, of course.

If you happen to live near salt water, you really have it made. We envy you. We lived on the coast of Florida for a number of years and know what seafood can be: Clams, oysters, crabs—I can't go on!

Those of us who are limited to freshwater fish are definitely disadvantaged but by no means out of contention in the
gourmet department. We do have trout, eels, and channel cats,
for instance. Besides, anyone can make a pompano or red snapper taste great, but it's an interesting challenge to the chef to do
something creative with, say, a carp. So look at it as a contest—
you versus the carp.

Carp, along with suckers and chubs, are commonly called
"trash fish" by people who don't mind slandering God's creatures and who won't take the trouble to learn how to cook them.
Truth is, if you cook them according to the usual cookbook
instructions, you'll soon learn *why* they're called trash fish.
Yech! It's a shame that such an abundant protein source is den-
igrated because of unskillful handling or prejudice. Here's an
interesting situation: People worried about protein shortages
are learning how to mix soybeans and grains together so they
shouldn't get amino acid deficiencies, while tons of high-qual-
ity protein—in the form of carp—swim about and are ignored in
almost every body of water in the country. I'll bet if we really do
get a serious protein shortage in the future, for every person
actually mixing those soybeans and grains you get ten who
learn to appreciate carp.

People also call them "scavengers" in a deprecating tone. But
these same folks will pay exorbitant prices to eat lobster or crab, the
most thoroughgoing scavengers of all. (When we lived in Florida,
Daddy used to ride to work with a real crab gourmet. Whenever he
saw a dead dog along the road he'd stop the car, run over and kick

the carcass till the crabs would scurry out and grab them up to take them home for dinner. Daddy was always being docked for lateness because of this guy's predilection for crab meat.)

The problem with trash fish is that they have too much moisture in their flesh. If you cook them in the ordinary way, they'll have a mushy texture, which is what makes them objectionable. I'll give recipes for them later.

Some people even call catfish "trash." Now that's going too far! Catfish, properly handled, are really delicious. Catfish are being raised commercially in the South now, so probably they will steadily gain in repute. There seem to be five distinct species of catfish in our local water. And while some are better than others, they're all pretty near gourmet food. Cats are the one genre of fish wherein the freshwater specimens are better eating than the marine. Catfish and eels are both fatty fish, which is what you keep in mind while cooking them. If you just stick them in a greasy frying pan you're going to end up with a greasy mess.

The other fish we commonly catch—bass, trout, crappies, and the various sunfish—are generally recognized as good eating, and any cookbook will tell you how to cook them just fine. We also occasionally eat freshwater mussels and crayfish.

Often we catch a fish with roe in it. A carp in our area might have as much as two pounds of roe in it. If the fish was in muddy water, the roe may smell rank, and then the chickens get it for a treat. Otherwise, fry it up like scrambled eggs or use it in other recipes (which will be forthcoming). We once made pseudo-caviar from sucker roe, and it actually came out good. When we tried it with carp roe, it turned out lousy.

Some people won't eat fish because they fear it may be polluted. That is a valid fear in our day and age. However, one must eat *something*, and the item you buy in the grocery store in a pretty package is about as likely to be polluted as that which you procure yourself. Wrapping it up in cellophane and putting it in a supermarket's display case never has caused pollutants to leave an article of food, though people act as though it does. In the case of fish you catch yourself, it helps to know your water. If there's contamination by heavy metals or other dangerous chemicals, you're almost certain to hear about it. If you suspect sewage contamination, you're perfectly safe if you cook the fish well. (You should cook fish well in any case because of certain parasites found even in fish caught in the purest water or bought in the poshest supermarket.) If you took your fish from water that just happens to look dirty or scummy, don't worry about it. We're fortunate in that the water here is part of a big city's reservoir system, and they take steps (such as putting up "No Fishing" signs) to keep it pure.

* Catching Fish *

First, keep in mind I'm talking about meat for the table, not sport. To me, catching a fish I don't want to eat is like flirting with a boy I don't want to date. What's the sense of it?

The old adage is that "10% of the fishermen catch 90% of the fish," but, contrariwise, when they're biting any dummy can catch them, and when they aren't even experienced fishermen do poorly. When it's marginal the adage rings truer, of course. We're in the 10% category, but that's because Daddy goes fishing about 100 days a year, and he'd have to be a complete idiot *not* to be an expert. (Don't worry about it. When you get into possum living you'll become an expert, too.) So let me wring out this veritable sponge of Wilderness Wisdom so that you too may put Meat on the Table:

* If they don't bite at one spot, go to another spot.

* If they don't take one kind of bait or lure, try another kind.

* If they don't take the bait sitting still, slowly move it.

* If they don't take the bait sitting still or slowly moving, move it fast.

* If they don't take the bait sitting still, slowing moving, or moving fast, throw in a stick of dynamite.

* When you catch a nice fish, kill it, then open its stomach to see what they're eating.

* Disregard the solar-lunar theory of feeding activity; it's complete nonsense (at least with respect to freshwater fish in our area, where we have thoroughly tested it).

* Fish do, however, feed in a cyclical manner. You often have an hour of activity followed by an hour or two or three of lull. These "windows" of activity can't be plotted on simple charts, though. Usually they will occur within a half hour or so of the time

that they occurred the previous day (either forward or backward), unless the water conditions change drastically.

* You might read that feeding activity is related to atmospheric pressure. But consider—how does that fish know what the atmospheric pressure is, after all? The pressure he senses is changed more by a few inches of water depth change than by the few psi the air pressure will ever change. This is a typical instance of how common sense will stand you in better stead than "expert advice."

* Three days after a heavy rain, or just as the mud from a flood condition is settling, is often a good time to fish—they're out looking to see what goodies have been washed into the water.

* All else being equal, you do better just at sundown than at other times. The daylight feeders are just going off duty, and the night shift is coming on.

* If the water is clear, you can walk along a creek and *look* to see where the fish are.

* They bite in cold water, but much more actively above 52°F.

We find all sorts of things to use for bait. In Florida we caught fiddler and hermit crabs. Sometimes fish would take fiddler crabs and ignore the hermits, and vice versa, showing how finicky they can be. Here we use worms, minnows, grasshoppers, katydids (good for blasé bass in the late summer), grubs, Japanese beetles, crayfish, hellgrammites (especially good), caterpillars, and aquatic insects (Things Found Under Rocks). Some fish are semi-vegetarian and you use kernels of canned corn or mush-balls of flour and corn dough to bait them. Carp are the prime example, but that elite sportfish, the trout, also eats corn. We use artificial lures occasionally, especially spinners. Often a spinner-worm combination will prove more effective than either the spinner or the worm used individually. If the fish are especially turgid, try a spinner-worm combination slowly jigged. Jigging means you make the lure dart ahead a couple of inches, then slowly flutter back. The fish think it's a food item being beset by minnows and come expecting to cop both the food item and the minnows—an easy feast. Fish have an instinct to ration their energy outlays and won't move unless you make them think they're getting a bargain. Sometimes, however, they go into a feeding frenzy and hit anything that moves. Even as the instincts of you and me are manipulated at auctions and bargain-basement sales, so we take fish.

Following are some unorthodox fish-getting methods. Most are illegal.

Take a large treble hook and attach it to a stout line, which is attached to a stout pole, such as a broomstick. The hook is tossed in where fish are schooling, then suddenly snatched through the water. Quite often you foul-snag a fish. Once, in Florida, Daddy got over 30 pounds of mullet in 30 minutes by this method. Or you can lower the line from a bridge or steep bank and move the line very slowly till it starts moving on its own. That tells you a fish is touching the line with some part of its body. Snatch it up! (Be careful not to pull a muscle in your back. Rehearse the maneuver in your mind, then you'll be okay.)

Daddy has shot fish with a pistol. The bullet doesn't have to actually hit the fish; the concussion of its hitting the water near the fish knocks it senseless, and you scoop it up.

People have been known to set off explosions under water to get fish, but this goes against our grain. We don't kill anything without eating it or else to be rid of it as a pest or health menace. We won't kill for sport or money (fur animals, for instance). We also don't take undersize fish or fish out of season.

"Monkey fishing" is a practice I've heard about but never witnessed. The leads from a hand-cranked electrical generator, such as a military field phone, are put in the water and the juice applied. The fish are stunned and float to the top. Apparently, the ones not taken recover unharmed.

Some people tie ropes to discarded automobile tires and toss them into the water in the fall. Then, when the weather turns cold and fish are hard to get, they pull them up by the rope and take out the hibernating fish. A five-gallon oil can with a 6-inch-diameter hole cut in the lid and small holes punched in the bottom works even better. The fish think it's a nice safe cave for them to hide in. The steel milk cans dairy farmers use work, too.

Netting is the most efficient and illegal method of all. The kids around here sometimes use lengths of chicken wire to corral fish in the creek. In Florida many people have throw-nets. Those are circular pieces of netting about 15 feet in diameter.

There's a small hole in the center and lines run from the outer edge, through the hole, and are held in the operator's hand. The outer edge is weighted. You throw the net into the water, let it sink momentarily, then pull up the lines. That brings the outer edge to the center, forming a pouch with the fish trapped inside.

Daddy made a bow of ash wood and some arrows and likes to go play mighty hunter with it. He did shoot two carp with it, though. When carp are spawning in the spring they're so vulnerable you can practically scoop them up by hand. (We actually have caught spawning suckers by hand.) Some people spear them with pitchforks at spawning time.

If there are fish in your local water, there are ways to get them out. Normally, fish are so easy to get that the ordinary hook-and-line method is sufficient for all you can eat, and is more fun besides. I've mentioned all those other ways to ease the minds of people who think they're going to starve to death if they don't have a job.

The first time I hooked a fighting smallmouth bass, and that thing ran the line all over the pond, leaping and all—just as in *Field and Stream*—I about peed in my pants with excitement. Talk about fun!

Daddy hooked a 27-inch carp once and got so excited trying to land it, he jumped in the water (it was cold, too) and ran all up and down the creek trying to reel up that thing. It's a wonder he didn't catch pneumonia to pay for all the fun he got out of it.

We tell people who have the Protestant Work Ethic and might resent us that we have to go fishing whether we want to or not, for food. But the truth is, we always do want to.

* Cooking Fish *

Before you cook your fish, you must first clean it (of course). Nothing to it. Unless you are going to fry the fish or broil it, you don't even have to scale it. If you bake it or cook it over an open fire, the scales will bake hard to the skin, which you remove, scales and all, when the fish is done. If you steam it to remove the meat from the bones, the scales will just wash right off.

Cookbooks always tell you to skin a catfish or eel, but we never do. It's one hell of a job for nothing. The skin comes right off the cooked fish, and it's not objectionable in any way. You don't skin any other fish, so why a catfish or eel? If you want, you can scald them in hot water (about 180°F) and scrape them with a knife before cooking. That removes the slime and coloring matter from the skin and leaves them white and clean looking—very esthetic.

The first thing to do with a catfish is to kill it. Unlike most others, a catfish will not die quickly out of water, so the humane thing to do is give it a sharp rap over the head. Then take a pair of wire cutters and clip off the spines in the dorsal and gill fins. They can give you a nasty stab wound.

Then, as with any other fish, you simply open it from anus to gills with a sharp knife and remove the innards and gills. Make your cut shallow so you don't mess up the roe. We usually leave on the head, tail and fins for the simple reason that the fish looks nicer that way; and it means less work. Also, many fish have considerable amounts of meat in their heads—just like some people.

69

Wet fish (carp, chubs, suckers) are the types preferred by some Jewish people for gefilte fish, but we haven't tried that, so I can't tell you about it. What we sometimes do with them is first soak them in a saturated salt solution in a bowl in the refrigerator for a day or two, and then cook them very, very slowly in the oven or outdoors over a hickory fire. The brine and the slow baking get the excess water out. When the oven is used to do the baking, we sometimes let it cook at a low temperature until the fish begins to drip freely, and then just turn off the oven and let it sit till the next day—remove the liquid and finish cooking. Sometimes we do it over a three-day period. No, the fish won't go bad, because the cooking will mostly sterilize everything, and new microbes won't get into the closed oven and start working that fast.

Usually, though, we make Chinese-style fishballs, congee, or eggrolls with wet fish. The fish is placed in a pot with an inch of water in the bottom and steamed for a few minutes. Rinse off the scales under cold water and remove the flesh from the bones. Sometimes we also steam the roe and use it with the meat in the eggroll and congee recipes.

FISH EGGROLLS

* Place 2 cups of flour (white flour or half white and half whole wheat) in a bowl. Stir in a pinch of salt.
* Make a depression in the flour and crack 1 or 2 eggs into it. Stir the eggs into the flour.
* Slowly add water and stir until a stiff dough is formed.

* Knead well.
* Roll out to a thin sheet on a floured surface.
* Cut into 6-inch squares. The trimmings can be gathered, kneaded, rolled, and cut again.
* Take chunks of steamed fish meat and roe (optional) and mix equally with chopped or shredded vegetables.
* Add salt, pepper, and celery seed to taste. A little filé sprinkled in adds an exotic taste. (Filé is the dried, early spring leaves of the sassafras tree.)
* Place some of the fish mixture on each square of dough in such a way that it can be rolled up and the ends pinched shut.
* (Optional) Seal by dribbling a stiff cornstarch-and water mixture on the edge of the rolled dough and ends
* Fry in oil until the dough turns light golden brown.

Good vegetables to use in various combinations are cabbage (or any cole), coarse lettuce, onion, chives, celery, parsley, bell peppers, green tomatoes, cress, or purslane—use your imagination.

FISHBALLS (BEST PART OF THE FISH)

* Add a small amount of salt, pepper, garlic, parsley, and/ or celery seeds and leaves to the steamed fish meat.
* Chop it fine or run it through a meat grinder.
* Stir, mash, and turn it in a bowl with a spoon till it begins to form a cohesive mass.

* Take a tablespoon full of the pasty mixture and knead it thoroughly until it can be rolled into a firm ball, with a surface that is no longer sticky (this is important for good texture).
* Fry the balls in oil. Serve them over greens and top with an appropriate Chinese sauce, such as cornstarch sauce. They also go with a sweet-and-sour sauce or a horseradish-and-tomato sauce.

WET FISH CONGEE

* Boil 3 cups water.
* Add 1 cup rice.
* When the rice is almost tender, add the fish meat and roe and some chopped vegetables. Add margarine. Good vegetables to use are celery, parsley, onion, yellow rocket, cress, or any cole.

A catfish (or eel) wants to be cooked so any excess fast can drip or be poured off but is still plenty juicy. We often stuff sage leaves or dill weed in the abdominal cavity and into cuts made in the flesh, and bake. Thyme and marjoram are good herbs to use, too.

CREAMED CATFISH

* (Optional) Partially cook catfish over a smoky fire, preferably of hickory.

* Put them into a pot with 2 cups of water and boil, covered, till the flesh will come off the bones—about 2 minutes.
* Remove and allow to cool. Save the water, and now call it "stock." Remove the meat from the bones.
* Put the bones, heads, tails, fins, and skins back into the pot with the stock and simmer 15 minutes. Pour it through a strainer, retaining the stock and discarding the rest.
* Add a cup of chopped celery to the stock and simmer it slightly. (The celery should still be crisp.) Then strain it, saving both stock and celery.
* Add $2/3$ cup of powdered milk to the stock, and stir well. Keep the stock handy and proceed to make a roux as directed below.
* Melt $3 1/2$ tablespoons of margarine in a large saucepan over a low flame.
* Slowly add 5 tablespoons of white flour, stirring constantly to mix well and to get rid of all the lumps.
* When well mixed, add about $1/2$ cup of the stock. Stir this in well and keep on stirring until you get all the lumps out. Turn the flame up to medium.
* Gradually add the remainder of the stock, stirring constantly, until it's well blended. Keep the heat just below the simmering point. If the sauce seems too thin, gently simmer until it's thick enough, keeping in mind that you will cook it some more.

* Add the meat, celery, dill weed, some diced onion, and diced bell peppers and stir. Gently simmer until the peppers and onions are just getting tender, about 5 minutes.
* Serve with paprika and wheaten cakes or toast.

SUNFISH (OR OTHER APPROPRIATE FISH)

* Use fresh fish. Salt well.
* Fry, almost poach, in margarine with a goodly amount of lemon juice and a little marjoram and garlic. Don't overcook.

SUCKER CAVIAR

* Remove the roe—tear the membrane so the eggs themselves are exposed.
* Prepare a brine of 1 cup salt per quart of water. You want twice as much brine as roe.
* Let the roe soak in the brine, refrigerated, 30 minutes.
* Strain the roe from the brine.
* Store in the coldest part of the refrigerator, in an airtight glass jar for about 2 months.
* Strain out any liquid, re-pack in glass jar, and keep in the freezer until wanted.

(The basics of the caviar recipe are from *The Joy of Cooking*, our favorite cookbook.)

MUSSELS

* Put mussels in a pot with an inch of water, and steam them to make them open their shells. Any that don't open should be discarded.
* Remove them from the shells. Cut them open and remove the stomach contents. Rinse well.
* Fry in margarine.
* Serve with your favorite sauce.

Sometimes we set each mussel on a half shell, add some horse-radish sauce, and chill in the refrigerator before serving. This is more a joke than anything.

Don't bother with mussels if you don't have a good set of jaws.

Crayfish taste great, but catching enough to make meal takes too long. It's fun, though, wading barefoot in a woodsy creek on a hot summer day, turning over rocks. The crayfish scurry about like crazy when you find them, but aren't too hard to grab. You cook and eat crayfish the same as if they were little tiny lobsters, which indeed they are. If you want efficiency, go work in some grimy factory and buy lobster—if you want to live right, go catch crayfish all of a summer's day. (Come to think of it, that attitude more or less sums up our whole outlook on economics.) Hint: The most and the biggest crayfish are found under bridges where pigeons roost.

* Turtles *

Turtles are very interesting creatures, at least to me. I was practically weaned on turtle meat. We lived in Florida then, and sly old Daddy was letting on that he couldn't find a job, so we would "have" to eat terrapin. The old phony!

Here we settle for snapping turtles since there aren't any diamondbacks. Five or six times a year in the warmer months we set lines for them. Snappers live anywhere you find ponds, lakes, or sluggish streams, even in cities. They're fairly common around here.

We usually set out eight lines at a time. These consist of a short length of cord of at least 50-pound test strength, a leader of 2 feet of very heavy monofilament, and a hook. Don't use a wire leader because it's stiff and the turtle can get a grab on it and snap it off. Monofilament is softer and gets caught in the corner of its mouth, where it can't bite as well. The hook is of a size that a snapper can get down its throat while a small turtle can't. Two inches long and $\frac{1}{2}$ inch across the bend is about right. Just tell the man at the sporting goods store what you want to do and he'll fix you up right.

Bait for snappers is easy enough. Any meat or fish will do, the rottener the better. Daddy uses fish heads that have sat out in the sun for a day or two. Small sliders (described below) and muskrats can bite off the bait without getting caught, so have a philosophical attitude ready about that.

Throw the baited hook into shallow water. Snappers

normally prowl about shorelines at a one-foot depth of water. They like the places where little rivulets might carry something their way, or else swampy ground which might produce frogs or birds. If you see signs of muskrats, forget it, because the snapper that is probably there will never get a chance at the bait.

Don't set your lines until the sun goes down or the sliders will get a free meal at your expense. Sliders are those smooth-shelled turtles that sun themselves on rocks or logs and slide into the water when you scare them. They comprise many species, all of which eat snapper bait without scruple and without getting caught. They are good eating and we have eaten a few, but it takes a pretty big slider to make it worthwhile getting it out of that hard shell. (If you do find a big slider, chances are it's not native—at least in the Northeast. It's probably someone's pet turtle from a pet shop that was freed. However, don't let that stop you from enjoying it.)

Tie the other end of the line to a bush or heavy rock. Usually we come back to check the lines at about 2:00 AM. Daddy says it's so we can take up any that are hooked before they have a chance to bite through the line, and to re-bait others, but the true reason is that he can't stand the suspense. We come back again at dawn.

Draw the line up slowly because sometimes the snapper will have a bite on it without being actually hooked, and may be reluctant to let it go. We usually take along a scoop net or an ordinary garden rake to bring up a turtle if it decides to let go. If you come back and find the line actively moving about, you have a catfish on. This is a consolation prize.

One thing we definitely avoid doing is playing games with snapping turtles. They can bite off fingers without too much exertion. The only safe way to grab one is by the tail, which is the one part of their anatomy their jaws can't reach. A bullet between the eyes calms them down somewhat because they can't see where to strike, but the jaws still snap. Like the proverbial chicken with its head cut off, snapping turtles have a nervous system which continues to operate automatically after the creature is dead (if you want to consider not having any brains left as being dead).

We learned this the hard way. One time in Florida we were driving along in our VW and saw a leatherback turtle. Mom stopped the car and Daddy jumped out and shot it in the head. Since the trunk was full he put the turtle on the floor on the front passenger's side. Well, a mile down the road the thing came alive and started snapping. Mom (who was driving) pulled her feet up to save her toes and the car was weaving all over the place. We were lucky we were the only car on the road.

Some people reportedly play "turtle roulette." They feel around in holes in banks where snappers retire during daylight hours, hoping to grab the thing's tail with their right hand and gaff it before it wakes up. I don't know anything about this technique. If you want to learn it, go to any rural town and ask for Lefty. He'll be happy to tell you all about it.

Sometimes people will look at one of those hideous reptiles and remember they have an appointment to be not hungry when it's to be served up, and offer their regrets—which leaves all the more for us. Turtles really are disgusting to look at, but they do make good eating!

SNAPPER SOUP

* Boil the whole turtle briefly. If you haven't a pot that large, put the turtle in the sink and pour boiling water over it. It will thrash about, so be careful you don't get scalded.
* Cool it off with cold water. Rub off the coarse outer skin. Pinch off the toenails.
* Turn it on its back. Cut through the narrow places where the bottom shell joins the upper. (Use a heavy knife and mallet.)
* Cut the skin where it joins the shell all the way around.
* Pry off the lower shell.
* Remove and retain any meat adhering to the shell.
* Remove and retain the liver. Discard the gall bladder.
* Remove and retain the heart.
* Remove and retain any eggs, ripe or unripe.
* Slice off the anus and slit from there to the abdominal cavity. Use a heavy knife to break through the pelvis.
* Cut the digestive tract and sex organs free of the meat
* Slit the throat lengthwise from jaw to stomach. Pull out the windpipe and gullet.
* Invert the carcass over a bucket and pull out the innards. Rinse off the carcass.

79

* Remove and retain the meat about the skull. Discard the skull.
* Cut the neck muscles and tendons free of the shell and spinal ridge.
* Grasp the neck in one hand and twist the shell steadily in one direction until they part company. Retain the neck.
* Cut the legs and tail free and twist them off.
* Remove and retain any meat adhering to the shell.
* Cut through the vertebrae on the spiral ridge (use wire cutters) and pry out the underlying meat. Discard the shell.
* Discard the yellow fat on the leg. (On terrapins this fat is green and is retained.)
* You may pinch off some of the skin. The more you retain, the more gelatinous the product, so it's a matter of taste. (This is the point where you proceed with the recipe for pickled snapper on the next page.)
* Put the legs, tail, neck, loose meat, and sliced-up heart in a kettle, add water to cover, and simmer 20 minutes.
* Add a cup of sliced carrots and/or diced potatoes. Add water if necessary.
* Simmer another 5 minutes.
* Add a cup of sliced celery.
* Continue simmering till the vegetables approach doneness. Don't overcook them.
* Add a cup of diced onion or, better yet, leeks or scallions

with their greens. Thyme, marjoram, oregano, and/or a
pinch of rosemary may be added.
* Simmer about 3 minutes.
* Turn off the flame. Add a cup of medium sherry (or
   equivalent home product). Don't ruin your turtle with
   that "cooking sherry" they sell in grocery stores. Let sit,
   covered 5 minutes.
* Serve with cold sherry and wheaten cakes or toast.

Sometimes, before adding the onion, leeks, or scallions, we strain
out some of the stock, then make a roux, cook it brown, and beat
in the stock to make a brown sauce. This is combined with the
other ingredients and the next steps continued.

Snappers are good pickled. When we had a car we would take
along pickled snapper on any long trip, as a nonperishable and
very refreshing snack item. The feet are best. You munch them
up and spit out the toe bones.

PICKLED SNAPPER

* Proceed with the snapper soup recipe up to the point
   indicated.
* Put the cooked meat into large-mouthed jars along with
   raw onion rings.
* Cover with pickling solution made of 1 part vinegar to 2
   parts water, with enough salt added to give a pleasantly

briny taste.
* Spice may be added. We like celery seed and cress
  (mustard) seed.
* Let sit, refrigerated, at least 48 hours.
* Correct the taste with vinegar, salt, or water—whichever
  is called for.

Any turtle eggs you may find can be used same as any other eggs. Some people say they're the best to use in cake baking.

The liver and undeveloped eggs may be briefly steamed, mashed, and mixed with mustard and/or mayonnaise to use as sandwich spread or dip. (Chicken liver and eggs are good this way, too.)

If you suspect pesticide contamination of the water you took the turtle from, you might better discard the liver. Snappers are pretty high up on the food chain, and the fat and liver might have concentrations of the pesticide.

Besides the turtles already mentioned, we have also eaten leatherback turtles, which can be cooked like snappers, and gopher turtles. Gophers are large land turtles (tortoises) found in the South. They taste like beef, but their eggs have an unpleasant rank taste.

Box turtles, those little orange and black tortoises with the hinged bottom shell, are not fit to eat. They can eat poisonous mushrooms and store the poison in their meat. They're too small to fool with, anyhow.

7.
Gardening

As with other subjects we've discussed, go to your library and read books on the subject. Unfortunately, there are so many books on gardening that at least some of them are bound to contain mistakes, so use your common sense. Some authors give the impression that gardening is some sort of complicated, esoteric art/science. Actually, mankind was successfully practicing agriculture even before metallurgy or writing, so how complicated can it be? My favorite gardening book is *Vegetable Gardening* published by Sunset Books, but there are also other very good ones.

One popular book advocates "mulch gardening"—meaning that you put a thick layer of straw (or hay) on the garden to choke weeds and conserve moisture. It sounds good, and the author certainly tells about it interestingly, but there must not be any rats where she lives. Here, they got to nesting in that straw and came up at night and ate everything in sight. They ate the tomatoes, sugar beets, squash—anything they could reach. What the rats couldn't reach, the mice climbed up to get. We tried to trap them, but with all that fresh produce they ignored the bait. We probably had the world-record slug population in that straw, too. Others who tried it told us the same thing happened to them. So no more mulching with straw for us. If you don't have rats or mice in your neighborhood, it might work for you.

This same mulch lady implies that if you get "witch grass" in your garden, you're a dead duck. Witch grass is a minor nuisance, true, but don't give up your garden over it.

Many gardeners conscientiously dig under the stalks and other refuse of their crops to return the nutrients to the soil. Okay, but you also return the next generation of insect pests to the soil. You do better to burn the refuse and use the ashes on the soil. If you must turn organic matter under, use leaves, grass, or corncobs that won't contain insects or weed seeds.

If you're into gardening at all, you know about composting. Composting consists of piling up weeds, garden and kitchen refuse, etc., till they rot. There are different techniques, and their various advocates get pretty worked up about it and swear the others are all idiots. Not to be outdone, I do now make an extravagant claim—to wit, I have the world's fastest compost heap.

It's called a rabbit herd. We give the weeds, etc., to the bunnies and they have it ready for the garden the next morning. Besides bunny and chicken manure, we dig in corncobs to rot. When we feed corn to the rabbits we give them the whole ear, and they leave the cobs. We have a heavy clay soil and the cobs improve the texture. Garbage and fish and animal innards go in, too. With anything like that, we bury it deep and put rabbit manure on top to keep dogs from digging it up before it has a chance to rot. Fat or grease should not go into the garden. Ashes from the wood burner go in, heaviest where the celery and peas are to grow.

There's a horse stable near here, and twice a year they offer all the free manure that anyone will haul away. I believe riding stables, and even some private owners of horses, frequently make the same offer, so it might pay you to look into this source of fertilizer if you have the transportation to handle it. If any circus stops by your area, you might be able to get some really exotic manure from them.

When we lived in Florida we had a sandy, poor soil that would scarcely grow even weeds, so we went to various fishing spots and collected the trash fish people had left and dug them into the soil where we wanted a garden. We did that in late autumn. We grew fine, fine produce from those rotten fish—mainly big, sweet cantaloupes. The garden was fenced so dogs didn't dig up the fish, which is what would normally happen. Some people in Florida grow produce in their septic tank's drainfield. You can certainly grow fantastic crops in a drainfield in sandy soil, but I don't know whether or not the practice is sanitary.

Daddy says that during World War II you could scarcely find a lot or yard where someone wasn't growing vegetables. Why then and not now? Actually, in some neighborhoods, even in big cities, you do find small gardens in front yards and even on built-up terraces or rooftops. It always makes me feel good to realize that others have an interest in growing food, even if circumstances limit their scope. So go dig a garden, even if it must be in your front yard. If the neighbors comment on it, tell them you're conducting socioeconomic feasibility studies or to go screw themselves, as your temperament dictates.

We have two gardens totaling about 1,600 square feet, which is about all two people can handle without mechanized equipment or draft animals. It's enough to supply most all the vegetables we can eat. Although we only have a half acre, our lot is long, narrow, and sloping. The bottom is cooler in the summer, warmer in the winter, and always damper than the top part. Some crops grow better there and others grow better in the uphill garden.

Our gardens really yield, not only because the bunnies have gone to so much trouble to make them fertile, but also because we plan them well. No sooner is one crop petering out than we plant another in its place. We start plants indoors as early as the middle of February and are still planting (kale, radishes, onions, garlic) in early September, so you see gardening isn't just a sometime thing with us. We also bring in some root plants (turnips are best), put them in dirt in boxes, in a south window, and let them produce fresh greens for winter use.

Besides the actual gardens, we also have a spot which can't be dug properly because of tree-roots, but still serves to grow horseradish, Jerusalem artichokes, and mint, just three of the plants that grow well without much cultivation. We have put in plum and apricot trees, grape vines, and blackberry plants, but they are still too young to yield much. Besides good old reliable Concord, we've put in one each of five different wine grapes. When we find out which one is most satisfactory for our soil, climate, and taste buds, we'll grow it exclusively. (Incidentally, Concord grape wine is artificially sweetened by commercial producers—to appeal to the Little Old Lady, soda-pop market—but naturally produced, it's good.)

The busy man's landscape motto is "Don't plant it if you can't mow it." Ours is "Don't plant it if you can't eat it." (Actually I have, against Daddy's wishes, planted flower beds.)

About the middle of January the seed companies start advertising and mailing their catalogs. Send for them all. You'll pick up many good ideas from them and they'll really whet your appetite for gardening. None of them have George Washington on their sales staff, so expect some stretchers, if not plain lies. We haven't tried them all, but have had best luck with Shumway (especially for herbs), Jung, and Burpee. Kelly Bros. nursery stock has been perfect in our experience and that of our friends. Their addresses are: W. Atlee Burpee Co., 300 Park Ave., Warminster, Pa. 18991; J. W. Jung Seed Co., Randolph, Wis. 53956; Kelly Bros. Nurseries, Inc., Dansville, N.Y. 11437; R. H. Shumway Seedsman, 628 Cedar Street, Rockford, Ill. 61101. We had some bad luck with Park in 1976. They have a nice catalog, and nicely packaged seeds, but we had very low germination percentages with many of them, despite the fact we're very careful starting our seeds. There were weevils in their seed corn.

When you're deciding which strain of any given crop to order, try to lean toward nonhybrid types so you can produce your own seeds for future use. You save money that way. Naturally you select your prime specimens for seed stock. Keep in mind that many seeds described as "hardy" want to be frozen and thawed a few times to germinate properly. We put them in labeled envelopes (after they're thoroughly dry) and put the envelopes in a waterproof jar and let them sit outside all winter.

Hybrid vegetables often have outstanding characteristics, but it just isn't practical for the home gardener to produce their seeds. Early corn is one hybrid we continue to buy because we really love garden-fresh corn and want it as early as possible. We took a chance with late frost last year and it paid off—we ate corn on July 10, which must be a near record for this area. You know it's summertime and the living is easy when you bite into corn fresh out of the garden!

To decide which vegetables to grow, go through the catalogs and consider each item offered. If your space is limited, you will want to pick and choose pretty carefully. Remember to consider the growing seasons of various crops, and try to get in two plantings in one space. For example, when peas are about done, we dig them out and plant late corn in their place. Radishes, being fast growing, lend themselves well to this. Some vegetables—potatoes, for example—are so cheap to buy it hardly seems worthwhile growing them. We've also stopped growing squash because the neighbors invariably overplant it and give away the excess. Corn in season is cheap, but we grow it anyhow because the flavor of the minutes-fresh ears is really superior to that of even slightly older ones.

You know what your family prefers, so I'm not going to tell you what to plant. However, I will suggest that you consider asparagus. It's easy to grow, always expensive to buy, and enjoyed by almost everyone. Its one minor drawback is that it takes two years to become established. Once it is established, though, it will produce for years. Then there are peas: If you like them, you want to try edible-pod, or sugar peas, or Chinese snow peas, as they're variously labeled. They're easier to grow, easier to cook, and we think better flavored than regular peas. They really yield, too.

* Herbs *

We grow many culinary herbs, and it's a mystery to me why so few gardeners do. They don't require much space or care, and the fresh herbs are usually so much better than the dried, overpriced product from the grocery store that you hardly recognize them as the same item. If you appreciate good eating at all, you should grow at least a few herbs. You have at your disposal maybe twelve to fifteen distinct flavors and aromas to experiment with, and the combinations are endless. Basil, tarragon, thyme, and dill are our top choices, now that we've learned about them.

We like basil so much we practically use it as a vegetable rather than as an herb. It can completely change a bland vegetable dish. Try this sometime:

*Steam diced squash.

*When done, strain the squash. Turn off the heat.

*Add margarine and salt, and sprinkle with powdered milk to take up excess water.

*Add a handful of *fresh* basil leaves.

*Mix. Cover pot and let sit 5 minutes for the margarine to melt and the flavors to blend.

*Serve. Taste. Oh yeah!

Basil doesn't want to be cooked much or it will lose its flavor. Add it after cooking the other ingredients, or use it uncooked, as in salads.

Basil and tarragon don't keep their distinctive flavors when dried, so we often put them in small jars of vinegar to keep them. The vinegars can be used in salads or sprinkled over fried foods, such as potatoes.

Thyme goes into all sorts of dishes: salads, soup, fried fish, spaghetti sauce—almost anything that takes salt takes thyme. We put it into margarine that we melt to pour over popcorn. (A word of caution about growing or using thyme [pronounced "time"]: You must make, and strictly enforce, a rule banning cheap puns, or you'll go crazy.) Thyme cooks well, dries well, and makes a good herb vinegar.

Dill weed, the tender growing little leaves, and dill seed are both good. Their main use is in pickles, of course. We also use them in fish, salads, ground with wheat to make wheaten cakes, and in any cream sauce.

We also grow parsley, fennel, chives, wild ginger, sage, anise, marjoram, rosemary, oregano, spearmint, peppermint, horseradish, and garlic. One side-benefit of possum living is that you can eat garlic most anytime without offending anyone. Fresh savories were disappointing, but we did find a few uses for the dried product. Most of these herbs call for only 4 square feet or so to supply all the average family can use, so really do try to find garden space for them.

There's nothing esoteric about growing herbs, though everyone seems to think so. Truth is, most of them grow like weeds. Here are a few minor pitfalls to watch for:

*True tarragon doesn't grow from seed, as does Siberian tarragon. So if you buy tarragon seeds, you're getting Siberian tarragon, which is a cheap substitute for the real thing. Unfortunately, tarragon plants are hard to find. We got ours from Kelly Bros. last year, but I didn't see them offered in their latest catalog. You might try your local garden-supply store. If they don't have it, they might be able to tell you who does.

*Horseradish is another nonseed producer, but many seed companies sell the roots. When we want fresh horseradish we don't dig up the whole root, as they tell you to do. We dig to expose as much as we want at one time and cut it off. The part left in the ground always grows a new crown after a while.

*Marjoram that we grew from one company's seeds looked and tasted different than another company's. I don't know what's going on here, but Shumway's was best. Oregano also seems to vary. You may have to shop around and taste-test.

* Garden Cultivation *

Different methods are advocated in different books. As with anything else, use your common sense.

Mostly, garden plants want their roots moist but not in standing water. Sandy, porous soil presents few drainage difficulties, but the heavy clay we have here is another matter. Many gardeners fail to dig deep enough, or else put their gardens in too low a spot, and one good rainy spell rots out the whole thing. We're fortunate in that our lot has a gentle slope southward and the gardens get both sunlight and drainage in good measure.

To improve drainage even more, Daddy trenched them once. It's a lot of work and you may not think it worthwhile. There are certainly many productive gardens in our area that were never trenched or worked more than 8 inches deep. Ours have been worked about 20 inches down.

How lazy old Daddy ever got up the energy to do it is beyond me. It took about fifty man-hours of labor to do the job on the entire 1,600 square feet. First you dig a trench along the top edge of the garden and carry that soil to the bottom edge. Then, using a pick, thoroughly break up the bottom of the trench, pulling out any big rocks. Then throw in any fertilizer or organic matter on hand. (We used rabbit and chicken manure, leaves, and corncobs.) Chop it into the soil with a shovel. Next, dig a trench alongside the first, using that dirt to fill up the first trench. You treat that trench the same, and proceed till the whole garden is done. Make the trenches run perpendicular to the slope of the

92

land—in other words, if the slope is to the south, run the trenches east and west.

There is considerable nonsense being disseminated today about organic gardening. We are organic gardeners ourselves, and for the most part believe in it, but not to the degree of fervor that some zealots work up. We don't need commercial fertilizers because of the bunnies and chickens, and we don't like the idea of buying poison, but we do notice some losses to insects and rabbits. It's not that much.

Organic fanatics have basically sound instincts and many practical ideas of real worth, but then blow their credibility with exaggerated claims. For instance, companion planting and deterrent planting. I've read that garlic planted as a border will deter rabbits, but I've *fed* rabbits with garlic tops, and they *loved* it. I've read that marigolds deter this, that, and t'other. I really like marigolds. I like their look and I like their heady odor, and I wish they really *did* deter Mexican bean beetles, but they don't. Then there's mulch gardening again. Okay, now I know you're not going to believe me, but I really and truly have read that gardens mulched with straw don't get insect pests. Really! If they don't, it's only because the rats nesting in the straw have eaten up everything and there's nothing left for the poor insects to feed on.

This sort of thing is just what I mean by making a big deal out of something simple and easy. I guess we're dealing with examples of the Dramatic Instance: For example, some gardener plants marigolds or whatever, and by pure coincidence no beetles show up that year—they had business elsewhere, or something. After that, you won't get the idea that marigolds deter beetles out of that gardener's head with a stick of dynamite.

Now, at risk of sounding like one of these bug-bugs, I'll tell you about two ideas that really do work for us. Slugs are a big nuisance here. We put out scrap lumber between the rows for slugs to hide under, then turn them over and squash the slugs with a stick. Then we put praying mantises to work for us. They completely wiped out some asparagus beetles that were troublesome. (I *saw* them eating the beetles, so it wasn't Dramatic Instance.) In autumn and winter you look for the mantis egg cases—those one-inch-long, brown, foamy-looking things they deposit on stems—and bring them home. (One spring, however, we forgot to put them out and the house was more or less crawling with little tiny praying mantises for a while—but no harm done.)

* Foraging *

Thanks to the late Euell Gibbons, one may now eat weeds without reproach. Our opinion is that most of them aren't worth fooling with, despite their new cloak of respectability. They provide an interesting change in the diet, but I'm sorry to say that they're never going to stave off starvation, as some doomsday writers suggest. Should doomsday actually arrive, and anything staves off starvation, it'll be dogs, cats, fish, long pig, and garden crops, not weeds.

Here are the ones we've found to be worthy of serious consideration:

* Yellow Rocket *

Despite the fact that yellow rocket was highly touted by Euell Gibbons, I've never actually encountered it on any dinner table but ours. Its virtues are that it's delicious, plentiful, easy to gather, and stays green in the winter, when other greens are absent. In winter look for it around the base of steep hills where there may be springs of open water even in freezing weather. We've actually found it still fresh and green under several inches of snow. In warm weather it gets tough and bitter, but by then other greens are available. You use the leaves and crown and cook them same as spinach. Or you use the tender leaves raw in a salad. The young stalks and undeveloped flower heads may be used like broccoli.

Yellow rocket grows as a low clump of leaves radiating from a crown on the central rootstock. The leaf consists of a long succulent stem with lobes of leafy material on it and the leaf proper at the end. (Technically, it's a lyrate leaf.) The stem is pale greenish-yellow in color. The leaf material is shiny green, about like spinach. After a freeze, some leaves turn dark, almost purplish green. A biennial, it sends up a flower stalk in its second year. Upon this develop the clusters of small bright yellow flowers that are commonly called mustard flowers. These give way to thin pods containing seeds all in a row. At this time the leaves change to a pointy shape.

Yellow rocket makes a good pickle. You process in a manner similar to sauerkraut, but it comes out tasting—believe it or not—like olives!

ROCKET PICKLE

* Gather and wash 2 pounds of yellow rocket leaves.
* Begin packing them into a quart jar. After each $\frac{1}{2}$ inch or so, salt them well. Use noniodized salt. Pack them tightly.
* When the jar is full, press the material down and stab a knife through it five or six times.
* If necessary, add water until the pressed-down material is under the liquid level.
* Put a small clean stone on top and force the lid down to keep the material under the liquid.
* Let sit about one week at room temperature. Some liquid may overflow, so allow for that.
* When gas activity is about over, remove the stone, press the material to release trapped gas, and top up with vinegar.
* Let sit another three weeks or so. After opening for use, keep refrigerated. It will keep for months.

Upland cress is almost identical to yellow rocket in appearance except for having more lobes on the leaf stem (four or more pairs). It's also smaller, as a rule. It isn't common here, so we took seeds from a wild specimen and grew them in our garden. Now they grow all over the place. When grown in cool, wet weather, the flavor is identical to watercress, though the texture is slightly coarser. We like it raw in sandwiches or salads.

Watercress does grow here, but in polluted water. We tried to transplant it to clean water, but it didn't take, alas.

Wild ginger is so good we transplanted it to our property, although it's so common it didn't make much sense to go to the trouble. It's a low-growing creeping plant with a dark green leaf that can best be described as a rounded heart shape. Technically, the leaves are somewhat reniform or orbiculate. They reach a diameter of 5 inches and will be on a stem of about 6 to 10 inches. Wild ginger has a rhizome of about $3/8$-inch diameter that's usually exposed on the ground. Often you find a number of plants growing all higgledy-piggledy over a large area of ground. You find them in damp, shady woods. If you aren't sure of the identification, snap one of the rhizomes and smell it. A warm, spicy (ginger) fragrance means you have it.

The rhizome is what you use. We often use it Chinese-style with fish, stuffing it into their cavities before frying them. You can chop or grind it to use, the same as commercial ginger. The flavor and aroma are best when the rhizome is actively growing new rootlets and shoots, so we often keep them in a jar of water, out of the sunshine, till growth starts.

In the springtime we enjoy the wild onions that are so abundant. We treat them just like ordinary scallions. The yellow part of the stem, growing inside the coarser outer layers, is especially good. We also pickle the raw bulbs in pure vinegar (sometimes they turn blue—no harm). Wild onions get rank when hot weather comes along.

Cattail shoots and roots are okay, but not what the back-to-nature set would have you believe. Besides, they're a nuisance to gather and prepare.

Burdock stems, Queen Anne's lace roots, day lilies, rose hips. plantains, and various potherbs are okay under good growing conditions, and we occasionally have them, but it's generally easier to grow their counterparts in a garden than to find and prepare them. I'll bet it takes 500 calories worth of work to dig up 100 calories of Queen Anne's lace roots.

Purslane grows uninvited in our garden, but we don't mind—it's great in salads after hot weather has made the lettuce bitter. Its succulent stems really make the salad look exotic and festive. It's also good steamed.

We gather wild raspberries, blackberries, strawberries, mulberries, and crab apples to make into wine or jelly. They're all fairly common, so it isn't much trouble, and it's a pleasure to me to be out picking them. The Old Fool says it's tedious, but I notice he manages to get his share—yes, and more than his share—of the wine and jelly!

We gather sassafras leaves in spring, when they're young and tender, and dry them for filé. This is the filé of Creole cookery fame. It's really exotic. We use it in soup, egg rolls, and scrambled eggs. It has the reputation of being an aphrodisiac—so watch out! It doesn't want much cooking, so sprinkle it in the food after most of the cooking is done. Dried and stored in closed jars, it keeps for many months.

The bark from the root of the sassafras tree is the source of the root beer flavor of the food industry, of course. We've experimented with it, but since we're not fond of sweets, that's all we've done.

Sassafras is that small, scrubby-looking tree with the three types of "hand" leaves. One leaf will have no lobes, like a closed hand. One will have a large lobe and a small lobe, like a mitten with a thumb. And one will have three lobes, like a hand with the second finger and ring finger spread, and the thumb sticking out.

There's an abandoned orchard in our neighborhood and we get peaches, pears, cherries, and apples there, free. None of the neighbors bother with them—they apparently don't consider food to be food unless it's bought and paid for in a licensed grocery store. In season we get all the apples we and the bunnies can eat, and all I can dry for winter use besides. (Choice apples they are, too.)

Hickory and black walnut trees grow like weeds around here, and we usually gather six or seven bushels of nuts each year. This year the weather was all wrong—the hickories failed completely and the walnuts didn't do much better—so we didn't get but a bushel or two. Fortunately we still have some left from last year. If you have no experience with these nuts, remember that they must be stored in a dry place for a month or more before they taste good.

Field corn and soybeans are grown extensively here, and the machines that harvest them often miss considerable amounts, which we go pick by hand. The farmers don't mind because it would just feed rats and crows or rot otherwise. They're mostly religious people and probably feel good about their fields being gleaned, as the Bible is full of exhortations to allow and encourage the practice. (There's a fellow geek in our neighborhood who gleans for his chickens.) Most of ours go to the bunnies, but some we grind into flour and sometimes we use the soybeans in other ways.

* Mushrooms *

We have a book for identifying wild mushrooms and make good use of it. We've discovered fifteen species of edible fungi in this area so far. We also discovered that poisonous specimens are fairly common—so don't fool around with mushrooms if you don't know what you're doing. The only way to positively classify a mushroom as edible is to identify the exact species. Blanket tests, such as seeing if they darken silver, are not safe. And remember, some types not only kill you, they do it in a pretty horrible way. So why risk that for a plate of vegetables?

When we discover a new type, we go through the book and identify it. If the identification is ambiguous or the species is listed as at all questionable, it goes into the trash the same as if it were definitely poisonous. If we think it's safe, Daddy will try a small portion and we wait 24 hours to see if Anything Happens. If nothing does, then I can eat it. (Daddy is allowed to kill himself if he wants, but I haven't yet fulfilled my Link in the Chain of Being.)

Some wild mushrooms are definitely superior to the commercial item for flavor, and many are at least as good. The different species have different flavors, of course.

Strangely enough, some taste quite different from others of the same species because of different growing conditions. The oyster mushrooms (Pleurotus ostreatus) we used to gather near Philadelphia were just about the finest eating you could ask for, and the ones that grow here, just 40 miles away, are so bland we don't even bother with them. (Incidentally, there's a fortune awaiting the person who figures a way to grow Philadelphia-type Pleurotus ostreatus commercially. We experimented with it awhile, but got only mixed results—not good enough for commercial production.)

We often find more mushrooms than we can eat, and then we dry them for winter use (see page 112). The meadow mushrooms, the type most nearly like the commercial ones, are so common we once gathered 23 pounds of them in one morning.

I'm not going to describe any edible mushrooms because I don't want it on my conscience if someone makes a mistake. Get a book specializing on the subject or find someone in your area who knows what's what. There are associations of mushroom fanciers (mycologists), so you might try to locate one. (Libraries have books listing organizations and clubs.) Be careful, but don't be afraid to trust the judgment of a recognized expert, because if he hasn't yet poisoned himself he probably knows what he's doing.

8.
Grain

Many people are not aware that human food is sold in feed-and-grain stores. We buy potatoes, wheat, soybeans, and rolled oats there. Rolled oats are nothing but oatmeal, same as you get in the grocery store. A 50-pound bag lasts us about two years.

When buying wheat tell the clerk it's for human consumption and must be clean. We have dealt with five different feed stores and all the clerks have been very cooperative about finding a good grade of grain once they know it's for people fodder. Prices vary, but retail wheat usually runs about $4.20 per bushel. That's 7¢ per pound. The best we could find in the grocery store for comparable value was Ralston Wheat Cereal at 47¢ per pound—up 571%. Wheaties, at 75 cents per pound, was up 971%. Granola was 93¢ per pound; and something called 100% Natural was 87¢ per pound, for a natural ripoff of 1,143%. Wouldn't you think someone would just crack some wheat and stick it in a box to sell for, say, 25¢ per pound?

Bread is usually 60¢ per pound and has a high moisture content besides. It's also difficult to find a commercial bread that tastes good, like wheat. We haven't bought bread in the three years we've had our grinder. The grinder cost about $19, and I calculate it paid for itself in twelve weeks. We got it from Nelson & Sons, Inc., P.O. Box 1296, Salt Lake City, Utah 84110.

For breakfast cereal we crack the wheat, cover it with water in a saucepan, and bring it to a boil. We do this in the evening. Then in the morning we add more water and simmer it about 5 minutes. Add sugar, margarine, and enough powdered milk to take up any excess water. Sometimes we add some cinnamon.

We often use wheat in soup, same as you'd use barley.

Instead of bread we have wheaten cakes. The wheat is ground to a coarse flour; a pinch of salt is added; water is added to make a stiff dough. We form thin cakes and lightly fry them. For sandwich bread we add some white flour, salt, and water; knead; roll out thin; cut to convenient shape; and fry very briefly. We put the filler on one half of the bread and fold the other half over it.

For variety we add some corn, dill seeds, or soybeans to the wheat when we grind it for bread. If the soybean-wheat dough sits in a warm place covered with a damp cloth for two or three days before cooking, the bread will taste a little cheesy.

If you are unaccustomed to coarse wheat, start out gradually to let your digestive system get used to it. Once you're accustomed to it, though, you'll love it. And it's supposed to be healthy for you. The Roman army conquered the world on a diet largely of wheat.

Soybeans are a cheap source of protein for the bunnies and occasionally for us, too. The price varies widely, according to supply and demand, but the last time we bought them retail they cost $7.80 a bushel, or 13¢ per pound. If you can't find them for sale you can order them by the bushel from P. L. Rohrer & Bro., Inc., Smoketown, Lancaster Co., Pa. 17576. You'll pay slightly more since they're seed quality, but they're still a great bargain. (You can really get taken buying soybeans at a health food store.)

We often sprout soybeans and have them as a vegetable dish. Soak them in warm water overnight, then keep them moist but not wet, in a dark warm place, for several days until the sprouts are about 2 inches long. Then put them into a large jar, cover with water, and swish them around till the husks break off. You can then rinse off the husks. Don't worry about it if you don't get rid of them all; they won't hurt you. You boil them briefly and serve hot with soy sauce or cold in a salad.

Daddy sometimes lets the cooked sprouts soak in the water they were boiled in for days at a time, till they get *really ripe*, like certain cheeses. He cooks them again before eating them with soy sauce. I abstain. Everybody likes soy snackies, however.

SOY SNACKIES

* Soak clean soybeans overnight. Use plenty of water— they swell to about three times their original size.

* Swish them around to break off the husks and rinse
  away the husks.
* Drain. Fry in oil, stirring frequently. It's tricky to get
  them just right—they should be very dark brown but not
  burnt.
* Strain off the oil (which can be reused).
* While still hot, sprinkle liberally with soy sauce.

After much searching we finally found a recipe for making soy sauce, but haven't had a chance to try it yet. The soybeans are cracked and soaked in water overnight, drained, and briefly steamed. Meanwhile, an equal amount of whole wheat kernels are soaked overnight, drained, and cooked in a hot oven till they just start to brown nicely. The wheat is ground to a flour, water added, and a stiff dough formed. The cooked soybeans are added to the dough and the whole thing is kneaded and formed into a sort of loaf. This is placed in a wide shallow vessel and covered with a saturated saltwater solution. The vessel is left outside where it will be exposed to the direct rays of the sun. (If rain threatens, cover it over.) In about two weeks, the brine will turn dark brown and is siphoned off. That's your soy sauce.

The potatoes you get at feed stores (roadside produce stands sometimes have them, too) are "seed potatoes" or "ungraded" or "irregular," but taste just the same as any other potato. A 50-pound sack costs only $1.50 to $4, or 3¢ to 8¢ per pound. Some of them (about 10%) will be unfit to eat, but you're still way ahead of the grocery store game. People object to them because they're hard to peel, but we never peel potatoes anyhow. Why peel a potato that's to be fried or boiled and mashed and not one that's to be baked? I don't know, either, unless it's just something people do, like skinning catfish. We do cut away any green skin and the eyes, however.

One good use to which I put these cheap potatoes is in making dinner rolls that are everything a dinner roll should be: light, chewy, and of good flavor, with no yeast taste. Two of their other virtues are that you can use up leftover mashed potatoes and that they are cheaper to make than other rolls.

POTATO ROLLS

* Make up 3 cups of mashed potatoes (skins and all). Or use leftovers.
* Stir in enough water to make soupy (medium thick soup).
* Add $\frac{1}{3}$ cup powdered milk, 3 tablespoons margarine, $1\frac{1}{2}$ teaspoons salt, and 2 teaspoons sugar. Beat well. (If any of these ingredients are already in your leftover potatoes, omit them here.)
* Gradually stir in 4 cups flour. You can use white flour or half white, half well-sifted ground wheat flour (give the middlings to the chickens).
* Dissolve a packet of dry baker's yeast in a little warm water and add.

* Stir and beat thoroughly.
* If necessary, add enough extra flour so the dough isn't sticky. Knead well.
* Place in a bowl, cover with a cloth, and let rise 6 hours in a warm place (75°–90°).
* Do not knead again. Gently roll out to a thickness of 1 to 2 inches on a lightly floured surface. Cut the rolls into whatever size you prefer. Separate them and gently place them on a greased cookie sheet.
* Let them sit at room temperature till they rise to 3 to 5 inches. (About $2\frac{1}{2}$ hours at 70°.)
* Bake in oven at 375° till done (about 35 minutes). Poke them with a toothpick to see that they're not sticky inside.

9.
Groceries

The main food items we buy at the grocery store are margarine, oil, tomato puree (instead of tomato sauce), sugar, salt, spaghetti, and, in winter, oranges. Except for the oranges, we could produce or substitute for all these things, but we would have to have maybe five or six people eating at our table to make it worth the effort. We buy the cheapest brand and largest size of everything. When I'm to do the shopping Daddy makes me eat a big meal before leaving, to avoid temptation.

With people becoming more and more consumer conscious all the time, it's not necessary to rehash all the little money-saving tips. You know to read those labels, to avoid convenience foods, to compare, etc. Mainly get out of the habit of assuming a higher price automatically means a higher quality. When we see any item we normally buy (that isn't perishable) at a reduced price, we buy all we can carry—it's like money in the bank.

When you go to the grocery store, don't forget to go out back and look for discarded greens for your rabbits. Do it even if you don't have rabbits. We have found whole crates of perfectly good cauliflower, cabbage leaves, and artichokes, to mention but a few, apparently thrown out for some really trivial blemish. Or, as in the case of the cabbage leaves, for no blemish at all. If you think a bunch of filthy bunnies get those goodies, guess again.

10. Preserving Food

In spring, summer, and autumn, we get our food so easily that we feel no need to store up for those seasons. We do preserve food for winter use.

We dry apples, mushrooms, and some herbs. We pickle some vegetables and other herbs. We can turtle meat, catfish, and carp. We simply store nuts, herbs, and root vegetables.

DRIED APPLES

* Rinse, core, don't bother peeling. Cut into $1/4$-inch slices.
* Steam the slices 5 minutes.
* Place the steamed apples on screens.

* Place the screens up off the floor in a dry, warm, airy place. (I use our attic.)
* They are done when springy. Store in a tightly sealed jar in a cool, dark spot. A little mold on the dried apples won't hurt. We eat them as a snack. They don't require reconstituting or any other preparation, so they're possum convenience food.

DRIED MUSHROOMS

* Meadow mushrooms dry well. Separate the caps from the stems and place both on screens.
* Place the screens in drying area. (Be sure it isn't too breezy or the mushrooms will blow away when dried.)
* Check every day. Throw away the wormy ones.
* They are done when shriveled up. Store in a tightly sealed jar in a cool, dark spot.
* To reconstitute, soak in very warm water.

DRIED HERBS

* Marjoram, thyme, rosemary, oregano, filé, and mint dry very well. Rinse the cuttings.
* Spread stems and leaves thinly on screens and place in drying area.
* They are dried when brittle. Store as for apples and

mushrooms. Note: The leaves are easier to strip from the stems when they are dry.

PICKLED HERBS

* Tarragon and basil are best pickled; they lose their flavor when dried. Loosely pack the herb leaves in a jar and cover with vinegar.
* Let sit at least 4-5 days. Store in a cool place.
* Take out leaves to use. Use the vinegars in salads. When vinegar gets low, refill jars.

PICKLED OKRA

* Wash and trim okra pods, leaving $\frac{1}{4}$-inch to $\frac{1}{2}$-inch stems. Drain. Prick each pod with a sharp fork to help pickling solution penetrate.
* Pack okra into hot jars with dill heads or dill seeds and sliced garlic.
* Boil enough vinegar and water to cover. Use 1 part water to 2 parts vinegar. Add 1 tablespoon salt for every cup of liquid. Add celery seeds and mustard seeds. Boil for 2 minutes.
* Pour boiling pickling solution over okra, filling the jars to $\frac{1}{2}$ inch of the top.
* Add lids and process in a boiling water bath for 5 minutes.

They are ready to eat in two weeks.

To process in a boiling water bath: Place the warm, filled jars in a pot of warm water with the pot water coming up at least $^3/_4$ to the top of the jars. A rack should be on the bottom of the pot so that the jars are about $^1/_2$ inch off the bottom (you can make one out of chicken wire). Do not let the jars touch. Place the jars' lids on *loosely*. Slowly bring up the temperature until the water is boiling. Start timing for cooking at this point. When cooked desired length of time, turn off heat and after 5 minutes tighten lids. Let the jars cool somewhat in the pot before taking them out.

PICKLED VEGETABLES

* Cut and slice vegetables. Put into jars.
* Boil enough vinegar and water to cover vegetables. Use 1 part water to 2 parts vinegar. Add 1 teaspoon of salt per cup of liquid. Add any spices you enjoy. Add a little hot pepper if desired. When doing red beets add 2 tablespoons sugar and a dash of ground cloves per cup of liquid.
* Pour the boiling liquid over the vegetables. Process in a boiling water bath (as in the last step of the pickled okra recipe above) until the vegetables are cooked. Beets take about $^1/_2$ hour; onions and peppers only a few minutes, or no cooking at all. Celery and green tomatoes sliced thin need no cooking. If, while cooking, the liquid level in the jars drops too low, refill to $^1/_2$ inch of the top

with vinegar. They are ready to eat in two weeks, but will keep at least five months.

JERUSALEM ARTICHOKE PICKLE

* Use Jerusalem artichokes that have been frozen and thawed a couple of times.
* Harvest them in winter or early spring. Wash and trim away the hollow parts from the artichoke tubers.
* Dissolve 1 cup salt in a gallon of water; pour over 1 gallon of Jerusalem artichoke tubers. Let sit 12 hours.
* Rinse. Place Jerusalem artichokes into jars.
* Add garlic, cress seeds, celery seeds, and 2 cups sugar to enough vinegar to cover artichokes (about 8 cups vinegar). Boil.
* Pour the boiling vinegar solution over the Jerusalem artichokes. Process 15-20 minutes in a boiling water bath. They are ready to eat in two weeks. Note: If, after a few weeks, a white milky substance starts to settle out, that's just the sap from the artichokes.

* Canning *

This is one area we have sadly neglected, mainly because we don't have a regular canner. Besides, we prefer vegetables preserved by pickling, and we produce fresh meat throughout the year. We do put up pint jars of fish and snapping turtle meat. Frankly, the fish isn't great. The turtle cans very nicely, though. We use our pressure cooker (still pot) even though it isn't recommended by the manufacturer for this purpose, since it goes to a higher pressure (temperature) than the recommended 10 psi.

We hot-pack the pint jars, leaving $1/2$ inch of air space, and put them on a metal plate that comes with the cooker, to keep them off the bottom. Seal the cooker and slowly raise the temperature so as to avoid thermal-shocking the jars. When the pressure reaches 15 pounds, we time it for 15 minutes, then let it cool naturally for 5 minutes before cooling with cold water and breaking the seal on the pot. The lids are then tightened and the jars removed to cool till the domed, self-sealing lids "ping." Canning is not the big deal it's made out to be, and if you can grow or get more food than you can use immediately, you should get into it.

We store nuts and sunflower seeds in our uninsulated attic. It's hot and dry up there sometimes, and freezing cold at other times, which seems to suit the things just fine. Hickory nuts and walnuts taste "green" until aged at least two months, but will keep for several years if kept dry.

Herb seeds such as dill, anise, and fennel store with no fuss at all. Just let them dry somewhat on the stalk, then put them into jars (on a low-humidity day) and seal. Don't wait until they're completely ripe and matured, as is recommended in many books, or you won't get the full body of flavor inherent in the greener seeds.

Salsify, sugar beets, turnips, and Jerusalem artichokes are dug up in the autumn or early winter and kept in a box outside for winter use. Freezing and thawing don't seem to harm them as long as they stay dry, although I've read that they do. This year, winter caught us out and the ground froze solid, like a block of concrete, before we got them dug up. They're going to be there till spring, I guess.

* Smoke-Curing *

Fish (or other meat) can be easily preserved for at least several weeks by brining and smoking. The idea is mainly to remove excess moisture. The salt and the smoke will inhibit harmful microbe activity in any case, but the removal of water is what guarantees the meat will keep. You needn't take my word for this, by the way—William Shakespeare himself will explain the principle to you. In *Hamlet*, Act V, Scene I, the first gravedigger says: "Why sir, his [a dead tanner's] hide is so tanned with his trade that he will keep out water a great while; and your water is a sore decayer of your whoreson dead body."

No less true of a tanner is a carp or other large fish.

To get out the water, all you need for equipment is a packing crate (about 3′ x 3′ x 3′) or a plywood box or something like that with four somewhat airtight sides and a top, two cinderblocks, and a grill.

*Position the cinderblocks upright so as to support the grill 12 inches above ground.

117

* Scoop out a hollow depression (6 inches deep) between them for a fire pit.
* Build a hot, fierce fire in the fire pit.
* Smother the fire with sticks of hickory, cherry, apple, or other hardwood (*not* oak, evergreen, or shrub).
* Put the fish on the grill. The fish should be gutted, de-gilled, sprinkled with salt in the cavities, but not scaled or otherwise fooled with.
* When the fire starts to come up through the smothering wood with actual flames, cover the whole thing with the box. To keep out the air if it's windy weather, pack loose dirt around the edges of the box where it rests on the ground.

You can now forget about it for a day or two if you want—it will preserve. When you get around to it, open the box, pour the water out of the fishes' cavities, turn them over on the grill, and relight the fire. You do this several times, till all excess water is removed. With practice you learn to judge when the fish are done by feeling their weight in your hand. Or you can break them open to look at the texture of the flesh. If you can't get around to dealing with them for some time, merely light a small fire under them every other day and then cover them and the fire with the box. This will preserve them indefinitely.

You don't have to worry about the fire getting too hot because the scales left on the fish will act as a shield to keep the meat from burning—same as if you'd "cleaned" them and then wrapped them up in aluminum foil to cook. The scales will also keep the grosser wood tars from getting to the meat. The smoke flavor will penetrate—the tar won't.

Sometimes, if a day or two passes between the initial firing and the second firing, *"enzyme action"* will work on the fish. This produces a "cured" texture and flavor, which I find interesting and which Daddy greatly enjoys.

"It is not rotten either!" he maintains. "It's all the same as curing a cheese or a ham! Go to the grocery store and check the price of a cured ham or a cured cheese, some time; it's all the same thing—enzyme action! If you think it's rotten, just leave your share for me!"

Actually, it *is* good. We strip the smoked, cured meat from the fish and pack it into jars with herbs and vegetable oil. A layer of meat, a layer of herbs, salt, vegetable oil, more meat, etc. Basil, dill, thyme, chives, and especially sage are the herbs to use. This will keep for several weeks without further ado, and with canning should keep forever, getting better all the while. Its best use is in spaghetti sauce, but we also have it in sandwiches, in salads, or plain.

I've read an authority who said that if you eat a ton or two of smoked fish a day you'll get stomach cancer. But he also says that drinking fresh tea soon afterward will cancel out the harmful agents (free radicals—whatever *they* are).

11.
Nutrition

At the present time a great deal is being written about nutrition. Now that poor old Adelle Davis is dead of the cancer she swore her diet would prevent, all sorts of people are scrambling to cash in on her game. I wouldn't venture to contribute to this monstrous mound of manure, this Niagara of nonsense, if it weren't for the fact that many people who are inclined to possum living are also inclined to be health nuts. I don't know why this is. We, too, are health nuts—I'm not knocking that—what I'm knocking is the idea of buying health at a health food store.

Some years ago, when I was still a child, we visited a young couple who were very strict vegetarians and health fanatics. They actually drove 400 miles round trip periodically and spent good money for "organic food," which they claimed gave them "super health." (They had a book to prove it,) We got into a wood-cutting project with them and they began wheezing and gasping and quit after two hours while old unorganically fed Daddy and I were just getting warmed up to the work. So much for "super health." They had another book proving that vegetarians acquire a placid, sanguine outlook on life. It failed to mention that Adolf Hitler was a vegetarian. Some placid vegetarian *he* turned out to be!

Athletes are often conned into buying health food, or "supplements" as they call it. When Daddy was into competitive distance running, various runners (Daddy included) experimented with vitamin E, cod liver oil, etc., but there was never any noticeable improvement in performance. In fact, one of the best runners in the area seemed to get most of his caloric intake from beer and bologna sandwiches.

One manufacturer of supplements made a practice of giving a supply of his products to all our Olympic athletes. Then if they performed well he claimed his stuff did the trick. The losers—who got just as much of it—weren't mentioned.

Two products this guy hawks are wheat germ oil for vitamin E and cod liver oil for other things. Many people take them both at the same time. Now, it happens that cod liver oil, among other fatty substances, destroys vitamin E in the stomach. When scientists want to study vitamin E deficiencies, one method used is to force-feed the laboratory animals with cod liver oil after each meal to be sure the vitamin E in the food is all eliminated. Why don't the health food people tell you this? I've seen all sorts of publications extolling the virtues of both vitamin E and cod liver oil with never a word that they shouldn't be taken at the same time. If they don't know about it, that proves them ignorant on the subject and not to be trusted. If they know but don't tell, that proves them unscrupulous and not to be trusted. One company actually packages fish liver oil and vitamin E in the same capsule. Probably others do, too.

Even respected authorities make statements on this subject that seem to be contrary to observed fact. For example, there have been generations and generations of tough, hardy Eskimos who never in their lives ate even one green vegetable, but despite that fact there are U.S. Government publications claiming humans should eat green vegetables twice a day. In one of his novels Max Shulman made a joke on this point: A kid is told by the school nurse about the importance of green vegetables, but his family never has them. So he solves the dilemma by eating a dill pickle every day. It's green, right? It's a vegetable, right?

Okay, if you can't believe the health hucksters, and you can't believe the respected authorities, whom can you believe? Why, you believe in your instincts and your common sense, of course. If you're normal and healthy your body will tell you what it needs. If you're not an idiot you know to get a variety of foods, and avoid overprocessed "junk foods," and not rely on stimulants to keep you going. (One of the nice things about possum living is that you do have time and energy to prepare and enjoy good food—you don't need to grab a cup of coffee and a doughnut and run. You're not too tired at the end of the day to have more than a martini for dinner.) If you aren't normal and healthy then possum living isn't for you and your nutritional needs are outside the scope of this book.

The point I'm trying to make is that if you're eating possum fodder (whole wheat bread, fish, garden fresh produce, etc.), you're bound to get all the nutrients you need without a special diet or spending a lot of money—so don't worry about it.

12.
The "Necessities Of Life"

"We're so isolated we can hardly get the necessities of life, and when we do, why half the time it ain't fit to drink" (old Appalachian saying).

I grew up to the music of a merrily gurgling still and can flatly state that if you use just a little common sense, "it" will always be at least fit to drink and perhaps even excellent.

As you read on, it may seem to you that I'm insulting your intelligence by telling ordinary, commonly known facts, but honestly, there's an amazing lore of misinformation, ignorance, and superstition on this subject, and even some people who make a pretty good brew don't truly understand the principles. I have a book on winemaking that contains statements concerning distillation, for example, that are completely absurd. Please read this brief glossary before proceeding.

* Glossary *

* Baker's yeast—a cultured yeast sold in grocery stores

* Campden tablet—a chemical, sold in winemaking shops, used to kill wild yeasts in must

* Denatured alcohol—alcohol that has been deliberately poisoned, usually with methyl

* Distillation—the process of concentrating and purifying an alcoholic beverage by boiling off the alcohol and condensing the steam

* Ethyl—the type of alcohol in every alcoholic beverage

* Fermentation—the action of yeast on a sugar solution as a result of which the sugar is converted to ethyl and bubbles of carbon dioxide

* Fortified wine—wine that has had its alcohol content increased by the addition of spirits

* Fusel oil—an acrid, oily, volatile substance commonly produced during manufacture of grain alcohol

* Gin—liquor made by distilling an alcoholic solution to which juniper berries have been added for flavor

* Juniper berries—small blue fruits found on some "red cedar" trees

* Malt—cereal grains (usually barley) that have been sprouted to convert their starch content to sugar and produce enzymes to convert other starch

* Methyl—poisonous alcohol made from wood or by chemical means

* Moonshine—spirits (liquor) made by an unlicensed still

* Must—technically, fruit juice or crushed fruit that is to be fermented; commonly, any sugar solution

* Off-fermentation—a fermentation in which other chemicals besides ethyl are being produced; they're harmless but may adversely affect flavor

* Spill-over—what happens in distilling, when the froth on the boiling must goes up the still-pipe and gets into the liquor, causing some cloudiness

* Spirits—any distilled alcohol

* Still—a pot for boiling that can be closed off except for a pipe leading away from the top. There's an arrangement for cooling the pipe once it's away from the pot. This section of the pipe slopes downward so gravity carries the liquor out the end. (There are also other types.)

* Vodka—liquor made by filtering spirits through charcoal

to remove all taste and aroma except that of the ethyl, and then redistilling. Traditionally made of potatoes, it is today made of other sources.

* Wild yeast—yeast that occurs naturally on the skins of fruit, on raisins, and in dust in the air

* Wine—fermented must

* Wine yeast—cultured yeast designed to ferment must; sold in winemaking shops

* Yeast—living microorganisms capable of causing fermentation; there are many species

Let's discuss the health aspects of drinking. Ethyl may be healthy, indifferent, or unhealthy for you, depending on many circumstances. I'm not qualified to tell you if you should drink or not and I'm not going to do so. If you do decide to drink, however, I can assure you that it makes no difference whatsoever whether that ethyl was produced in a commercial operation or in your kitchen. If it's ethyl, it's ethyl.

Once a guest of ours, who does drink liquor, refused to touch a drop of our good product on the ground that it might be "impure." Well, Daddy has been drinking it pretty steadily for eighteen years now, and he can still run ten miles in less than an hour, so I don't guess it's harmed his body, and he still plays a fair game of chess, so I don't guess it's harmed his mind—so what is the harm? Our guest didn't know, either, but he still wouldn't drink any.

Daddy says overindulging (getting drunk) with commercial

whiskey gives him a headache next day every time, but our liquor never does. I don't drink enough to know, but others who've tried ours swear the same thing.

There are four reasons why home-produced alcohol has a bad reputation: First there are those bums who drink denatured alcohol and go blind or worse. There's a persistent myth that one or another process such as filtering through bread will remove the poisonous methyl. There are bums who actually do this, drink the stuff up, get drunk on it, and have no bad effect. The filtering business didn't do a thing, however. It happens that by a quirk of nature about 10% of mankind are able to safely metabolize methyl. Unfortunately, 90% of those who imitate them are in for big trouble. Methyl is produced by an entirely different process, and you can't accidentally make it while trying to make ethyl.

Then there are those ignorant or unprincipled moonshiners who use soldered parts in their stills. The liquor picks up minute quantities of lead which can accumulate in the human body to reach toxic levels. Stills should be designed so that the solution, the steam, and the liquor never come into contact with any metal other than aluminum, copper, or stainless steel. Also avoid plastics that may be alcohol soluble.

The third reason is that it's pretty hard to make "corn squeezin's," the traditional drink, without at least some off-fermentation, especially of fusel oil (see Glossary, above). In commercial production the aging process eliminates it, but moonshiners often neglect that step. Fusel oil has a really nasty taste and is the main reason why half the time "it" ain't fit to drink. This problem is easily bypassed by simply using refined sugar or sugar beets instead of grain, as they don't seem to produce fusel oil.

Fourth, it's human nature to equate value with cost. However, the reason commercial liquor costs about ten times what it costs to make moonshine has nothing to do with value. A quart of liquor would cost about the same as a quart of rubbing alcohol if it wasn't for the taxes.

✳ Yeast ✳

We get warm vibes from yeasts. When we inoculate a batch of must and the bubbles start coming up, Daddy is wont to say, "See, our little friends are in there doing valiant labor on our behalf. Let's drink to that!" Yeasts and humans have a true symbiotic relationship, I believe. There would definitely be fewer alcohol-making yeasts alive if it weren't for mankind, and I believe there would also be fewer people if it weren't for yeasts. There are many, many people who would never have been born at all if it weren't for yeasts. (Their parents got drunk.) If that doesn't constitute a symbiotic relationship, then *I* don't know what a symbiotic relationship is.

For practical purposes yeasts may be categorized as baker's yeast, wine yeast, or wild yeast (see Glossary, pages 125–27).

Fleischmann's active dry yeast is the type of baker's yeast we often use. Baker's yeast has the reputation of being lower class by the snootier home brewers, but we consistently get good results with it. It's cheap, fast acting, and reliable, which is more than can be said for many inoculation methods. Its main drawback is that it's hard to get it to work up a product of more than 10% alcohol content. This is no big deal in distilling, but we would like a little more in our wine.

Wine yeast is a bit more expensive and a bit slower acting but will work up to 14% alcohol without much trouble. The percentage of alcohol that can be fermented in a solution is limited by the fact that the yeasts are killed by a given concentration of alcohol. Those tales concerning the potency of "Granpaw's Old Juice" are interesting and often pretty funny, but if Granpaw didn't distill it or freeze-concentrate it (we'll discuss that later), it still wasn't stronger than 14%.

Grapes are the one fruit I might risk fermenting with their wild yeast. With most other fruits it's quite likely that you'll get off-fermentation if you try it. Many wild yeasts are very slow acting and incapable of fermenting up to a worthwhile percentage of alcohol. Some home-brew recipes call for raisins as the yeast source, but you're not likely to get good results with them.

Yeasts like a temperature between 65°F and 90°F, with minimum variation. They need nutrients other than sugar and water to work, but this isn't the big deal it's often made out to be. Fleischmann's yeast will work with nothing more for nutrients than the culture medium it comes packaged with. We've distilled gallons and gallons of ethyl made of sugar, water, Fleischmann's yeast, and nothing more. We do usually add a few ounces of boiled cracked wheat and tea to speed it up, though. Tea supplies tannic acid, a useful nutrient. It gives the must a bitter taste, but the bitterness doesn't go up the still-pipe. Wine yeast gets along well with the natural nutrients found in even a small amount of fruit juice or pulp.

We've tried culturing our own yeast and found it to be more trouble than it's worth. You have to sterilize your must with Campden tablets or by boiling. (If you boil it, be sure to allow it to cool to about 110°F before adding your yeast or it will be killed, too.) You have to keep your containers clean and take elaborate precautions to exclude wild yeasts. Sooner or later the wild yeasts do get in or the others mutate; then you gradually get more and more off-fermentation with each batch and have to start over from scratch. To do it, of course, you simply use a small portion of an actively fermenting batch to inoculate a fresh batch of must. Believe me, it's not worth the trouble.

The clerk at the winemaking shop will try to sell you a device called a waterlock, which you need if you intend to cultivate your own yeast but not otherwise. It allows carbon dioxide to escape from the must while keeping out the dust that carries wild yeast spores. The one or two wild yeasts that may get in aren't going to do a thing compared to the millions of cultured ones you've added, so why bother with it?

The chlorine that's added to municipal water supplies may inhibit or even kill yeast, so I've heard. (We have well water.) The remedy is to let the water stand 24 hours before making up the batch, or else boil it briefly and let it cool before proceeding.

* Sugars *

Any sort of sugar or starch can be used to make ethyl. Of course, starch must first be converted to sugar—unconverted starch won't ferment, though it will rot.

For our purposes we'll consider fruit sugar, refined white sugar, and sugar beets. I've heard of people fermenting home-grown sorghum but have no first-hand knowledge of it.

Many fruits have considerable amounts of sugar in them and can be used without other sugar being added. Others have less and should have more added. When making fruit wines you do well to make at least half the must of sugar water. If you make it entirely of fruit, you will have a hard time getting the sugar content right. Apples and pears, being somewhat bland, might be two exceptions to the rule.

Following is a list showing approximate sugar content of various fruits. The percentages shown are of the usable (edible) portions. Keep in mind that the fruit must be dead ripe to have maximum sugar content and that other factors also figure in. You can taste, say, an apple, and judge if it's more or less sweet than the average apple.

Apple 15%
Apricot 13%
Banana 23%
Blackberry 11%
Cherry (sweet) 17%

Grape ....15%–35% (taste them)

Orange 11%

Peach 11%

Pear 15%

Persimmon 33%

Plum 11%

Raspberry 13%

Strawberry 8%

Sugar beet 17%

I'll explain how to use this list on page 141.

Some people use canned or frozen fruit juice or syrups from the grocery store. These may or may not have something on their labels to give you an estimate of their sugar content. Be sure they contain no preservatives or the yeast won't work. Also check the price, since they're almost always expensive.

White sugar is by far the easiest to use, besides being relatively inexpensive and pure. At $1.29 per 5-pound bag, the current price in our area, the sugar needed to make a fifth of 100-proof liquor costs 43¢. A gallon of 14% wine takes 52¢ worth of sugar. You can save a few pennies by using other sources, but it hardly seems worth the trouble. Of course, you need some fruit for flavor and nutrients in the case of nondistilled beverages.

If you want to go the whole possum, you can grow sugar beets and make your must from them. Once when the price of sugar shot up we did so, but since it takes about 20 square feet of land to grow the equivalent of 5 pounds of refined sugar, we probably still came out behind because of the lost garden space. It's a lot of trouble, too.

Whatever the source of the sugar may be, it's all subject to the same basic principles. The amount of alcohol in the fermented product is directly proportional to the amount of sugar used, up to the limit of the yeast's ability (10% alcohol for baker's yeast, 14% for wine yeast). One pound of sugar in a gallon solution will ferment to a 6.3% alcohol solution, 2 pounds to the gallon will go to 12.6%, and so forth. (I refer here to a U.S. gallon of 128 fluid ounces. There are several books out on winemaking that use the British gallon as the unit of measure. Also, many handed-down-from-Grandmom recipes use a British gallon. A British gallon is one pint larger than ours.)

If you add more sugar than your yeast can handle, it will still go to its limit but you will have unfermented sugar left in the solution. The limit of Fleischmann's dry baker's yeast will be reached when you use 27 ounces of sugar in a gallon solution. This is a fortunate coincidence because distributing 5 pounds of sugar among three one-gallon jugs gives you just those proportions. The limit of wine yeast is reached with 35.5 ounces in the gallon.

You can buy a hydrometer to measure sugar content, but we find we get good results by weighing and estimating. If you buy one, have the sales clerk explain how it's used. If you don't have a scale to weigh out the sugar, you can get close enough by measuring. A level cup of granulated white sugar will be very close to 8 ounces.

* Equipment *

For winemaking you can get by with nothing more than the usual kitchen utensils plus a few ordinary gallon jugs such as those in which vinegar or cider are sold. We have about ten such jugs for fermenting vessels and some quart bottles for decanting. Of course, if you are going to be fanatical about letting your wine settle out perfectly clear, that will take time and your vessels will be tied up, so you might want more. Many home operators use five-gallon spring water jugs. Any sort of container that can be closed up reasonably well to keep out fruit flies and air will serve. Be sure to remember never to close a fermenting vessel completely airtight or the carbon dioxide gas pressure might build up to the bursting point.

We have a "fermentorium," as the Old Fool calls the packing crate we put the jugs into for warmth, but if your house stays reasonably warm, you won't need one. Inside the crate there's a socket for a 60-watt bulb which is wired through a thermostat set at 80°F. The thermostat came from a junked electric space heater. Ordinary batting insulation and a blanket thrown over keep the heat in. It works pretty well.

To distill, of course, you must have a still. The pot of our still is a six-quart Mirromatic pressure cooker. (We get triple duty out of it, using it as a still, canner, and pressure cooker.) The pipe is an 8-foot length of ordinary $5/8$-inch copper tubing. It's bent at one end like a shepherd's crook so that after coming straight out of the top of the pot it slopes around to let the condensed product run out to the end. For cooling, a 5-foot length of 1-inch copper tube was put over the other tube, the ends cut and bent and sealed with solder. Two nipples of $5/8$-inch copper tubing were soldered over holes drilled in the opposite ends of the water jacket. Rubber tubes (from a junked washing machine) were slipped into the nipples and taped up watertight. The end of the bottom hose has one of those rubber things that slip over a water faucet. The end of the top hose goes into a drain. We once had a still which had a bicycle inner tube as the water jacket. The input and output tubes were sealed in with putty and tape. Some condensers consist of a coil of copper tubing cooled by air, but they are harder to make and don't work as well. Sometimes, instead of draining the water down the sink, we'll attach the output tube to the garden hose and run it down to the garden.

A wooden support holds the pipe in place. (See illustration.)

Notice that the product doesn't come into contact with the solder.

Here's how it works: The pot is set on a burner on the kitchen stove, and the fermented must is strained into it. (The wheat and yeast residue is given to the rabbits.) Don't overfill the pot—two-thirds full is a maximum. The lid with its rubber gasket is then closed on it. A stiff dough of flour and water is mixed and spread around the nipple on the pot's lid, care being taken to avoid getting any in the hole. The end of the $5/8$-inch pipe is put over the nipple and seated in the dough, and more dough is spread at the junction to complete the seal. (This dough bakes hard during the

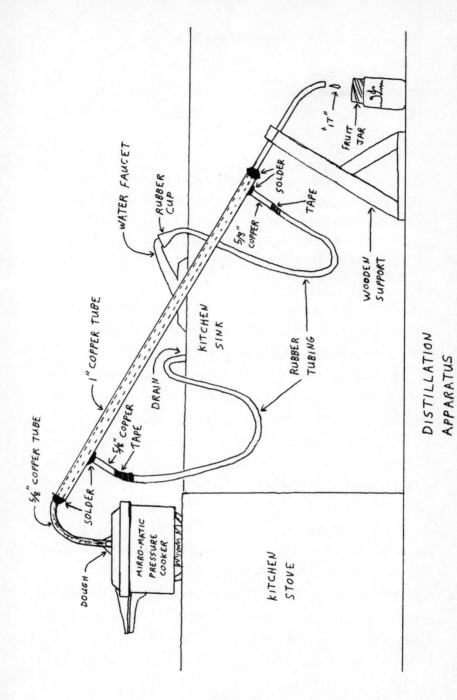

DISTILLATION APPARATUS

WATER FAUCET

RUBBER CUP

1" COPPER TUBE

5/8" COPPER TUBE

SOLDER

5/8 COPPER TAPE

DRAIN

KITCHEN SINK

RUBBER TUBING

5/8" COPPER

SOLDER

TAPE

"IT"

FRUIT JAR

WOODEN SUPPORT

DOUGH

MIRRO-MATIC PRESSURE COOKER

KITCHEN STOVE

137

run and is also fed to the bunnies.) The water hose is hooked up, the flame turned on, and that's it. With practice you learn to regulate the flame and water flow efficiently.

The first few ounces of the run will be within a few percentage points of being pure alcohol. As the run progresses, the alcohol coming through the pipe will have more and more water in with it. When a sample taken from the dripping pipe no longer tastes of alcohol, the run is over—all the alcohol in the must is now either in the fruit jar you set under the pipe, or in your tumtum. A gallon of 10% must will normally run out a quart and a half of 26.7% strength. Sometimes we'll take two of those runs and redistill them to get two-fifths of a gallon of 50% (100 proof) strength, or two quarts of 40% (80 proof) liquor.

Then again, sometimes we just go ahead and drink up the first run. It mixes well with anything gin or vodka mixes with. We like it with weak iced tea with mint leaves or anise seeds, but you'll soon find your own favorite mix. If you like gin and tonic, you're sure to like quinine-and-shine.

Since the first run is less than 30% alcohol (if you let the latter portion mix in with the stronger first cut), you can sip it neat, traditionally out of the fruit jar. If you do, you soon become a member of the Fraternity of the Ridged Nose. The ridge comes from the edge of the jar pressing the bridge of your nose as you put away the old juice. There are Ridge-Nosers all over the country. Don't try ridge nosing the first few ounces of the run or any of a double-run or you might find yourself on the floor.

Normally a double-distilled product will be as clear as

water (or gin or vodka, for that matter), but a first run might have some cloudiness due to spillover or frothing. If that bothers you, just let it stand in the refrigerator for a day or two and it will all settle out.

If you don't rinse out the still-pipe and let it sit a few days between runs, you may notice a film forming on the product toward the end of the run. This is "mother of vinegar" and is completely harmless. It's caused by vinegar-forming microbes which were at work on the residual alcohol in the pipe.

Incidentally, our small, efficiently cooled still gives off no tell-tale odor.

* Freeze-Concentrating *

You can raise the percentage of alcohol in a fermented solution by partially freezing it and then discarding the ice. Since water freezes at a higher temperature than alcohol, the ice will be mostly water. The main drawback here is that any sediment or dissolved substances, such as unfermented sugar, will remain in the beverage. This is not the case with distilling. On the other hand, freeze-concentrating will intensify the flavor of a bland wine.

* Winemaking *

Strangely enough, it's more difficult to get quality in wine than in moonshine. We can easily match store-bought vodka, for instance, but a good wine takes patience. (We generally drink it up before it ages properly, if you *must* know.)

We've made wine of Concord grapes that was fine, fine, mighty fine! Apples tend to make a smooth but bland product. Crab apples that have been frozen are very good. Strawberries, raspberries, and blackberries are good, but if they aren't absolutely dead ripe they will have a certain harshness when fermented. Peaches make a good wine but have a tendency to off-fermentation (see Glossary, page 126), so be sure to kill the wild yeasts before proceeding. Elderberries make an excellent wine. You must take heed of their ripeness same as with the other berries. We made rosehip wine once but it turned out acrid.

Dandelion wine, everybody's favorite, is a bit tricky. We've had good luck and bad luck with it. Having a still takes some of the sting off the bad luck batches, as we run it through to make Dolly's Delightful Dandelion Dew. I guess there are variations in dandelion flowers same as in any other botanical material. Dandelion flowers should be picked when they first develop and open, preferably in early spring. Gather them first thing in the morning before bugs get into them. Avoid getting any stems or milky sap in the must.

Okay, so suppose you have your fruit ready and are rarin' to go. In the case of apples or stone fruits you first remove the seeds or stones. Then weigh the fruit. If you don't have a scale, mash up the fruit (a necessary step anyhow) and put juice and pulp into containers and estimate the weight. The rule "A pint's a pound the world around" will be close enough. Thus a gallon will be 8 pounds.

Now that you know how much you have, decide how much must to make. For most fruits you aim at about twice as much must as you have volume of fruit. Make it come out even according to the fermenting vessels you have on hand—you don't want partially filled vessels since the air space will encourage the growth of vinegar-forming microbes.

Next, look up the fruit on the sugar list (pages 132–33) and note its average percentage. If your fruit seems more or less sweet than average, adjust the figure a point or two. Now you can figure how much sugar to add. The equation is:

$$S = .02 \times A \times T - (.01 \times W \times P)$$

Where: S = the sugar to be added, in ounces

A = the alcohol percentage your yeast can work

T = the total amount of must you want, in ounces

W = the weight of the fruit, in ounces

P = the percentage of sugar in the fruit (from chart)

Example: Suppose you have 7-$\frac{1}{2}$ pounds (120 ounces) of pitted plums and decide to make 2 gallons (256 ounces) of 14% wine. The chart lists plums at 11% sugar, so:

$$S = .02 \times 14 \times 256 - (.01 \times 120 \times 11)$$
$$\text{or } S = 71.68 - 13.20$$
$$\text{or } S = 58.48$$

So you add 58 ounces of sugar to the plums. (Three pounds, ten ounces.) Add water to make up your 2 gallons. Don't add all the

141

water at once, though, or the containers will overflow when the yeast gets working. Fill them $^3/_4$ up, and in a day or two, when initial foaming has subsided, you can fill them up completely. When the must has been fermenting about a week, you can strain out the pulp and again top up with water.

If you prefer, you can add more sugar than the yeast can handle, which will give you a sweet wine. However, if you wait to add the extra sugar till after fermentation is done you have a better chance of getting it just right. If you accidentally add too much sugar, you can dilute the wine with water, add more yeast, and ferment out the excess. Or you can distill it. But don't freeze-concentrate it or it will get sweeter yet.

Once you have your must made up, you can sterilize it or not, as you see fit. (To sterilize the must, add Campden tablets or boil it, but let it cool before adding yeast.) Then add the yeast and set it in a warm place to ferment. That will take 10 to 25 days, depending on circumstances. You know it's done when the bubbles stop coming up and it begins to clear and no longer tastes sweet.

If you want your wine to be perfectly clear, it must settle out, and that takes time. Some people add chemicals from the wine-making shop to speed settling, but I know nothing about that. Natural settling proceeds fastest if you decant into tall bottles and store in a cool place. Then you siphon it out, being careful not to disturb the sediment. You can get plastic tubing for a siphon at any hardware store. If the fruit contained much pectin, and you boiled the must, the wine will have a slight haze which never will settle out. I don't know why this should bother anyone, but apparently it does. When you decant, be sure fermentation is really over, or else cap the bottles loosely or they might burst. We usually add some spirits to assure that the alcohol level is definitely high enough to kill all microbes. This makes fortified wine.

* Recipes *

BASIC MOONSHINE MUST

* Have ready 3 reasonably clean 1-gallon jugs.
* Weigh out or distribute among them 5 pounds of white sugar. (Optional) Add a few ounces of boiled cracked wheat and the water it was boiled in and a little tea.
* Fill ³⁄₄ up with water.
* Add one packet of Fleischmann's dry yeast to each jug.
* Stir. Let sit in a warm place (80°F optimum) 24 hours.
* Stir. When foaming subsides, top up with water.
* Ferment.
* Distill.
* Enjoy!

VODKA

To make vodka, you first make charcoal. (Don't use that crap they sell for barbecuing.) You don't need much. We chop up some dry, dead hardwood and put it in a one-quart pot or tin can or something that can be sealed up almost airtight. Wrapping it up in aluminum foil works if you don't puncture it or make the fire hot enough to melt it. It's then put in a fire to cook out. For vodka it must be thoroughly cooked out, but if it still has a pungent smell to it, it will give the liquor an interesting whiskey sort of taste.

* Mix 3 quarts of ordinary moonshine with about 1 quart of cool charcoal. Stir. Let sit 24 hours.
* Flush out the still-pipe with a garden hose.
* Strain out the charcoal. (Use an ordinary strainer; small particles left in won't matter.)
* Distill somewhat slower than usual.

GIN

* Gather juniper berries. They must be dead ripe (pure blue and soft) or they'll impart an unpleasant resinous flavor. You get them in late autumn and winter.
* Put 6 tablespoons of berries in the still-pot and slightly bruise them. (Don't crush them.)
* Add 3 quarts ordinary moonshine. Stir. Let sit 2 hours.
* Flush out the still-pipe with a garden hose.
* Distill somewhat slower than usual.

SUGAR BEET LIQUOR

* Slice thin or mince into a kettle 10 pounds of sugar beets.

* Add just enough water to cover and bring to a boil.
* Simmer 15 minutes, stirring occasionally. Strain off this liquid and retain. Retain the pulp.
* Repeat the previous three steps to the pulp.
* Discard the pulp. (Give it to the bunnies.)
* Combine the liquids and simmer until the steam no longer has a rank odor.
* If the liquid is less than a gallon, add water to make it so. If it's more than a gallon, boil it off till it is.
* Cool to below 110°F, and add one package Fleischmann's yeast.
* Ferment.
* Distill.
* If it tastes too beety, make vodka of it. (See above.)

DANDELION WINE

* Pick 1 gallon of loosely packed dandelion flowers, avoiding the stems and sap. You just want the yellow petals.
* Pour actively boiling water to cover. (Think: Will your container stand the thermal shock?)
* Cover and let sit 4 days. Stir once a day.
* Strain the liquid into a 1-gallon jug.
* Add the juice of 2 oranges. (Some people add the whole fruit—skin, pulp, and all. We suspect the skin of some oranges may cause bitterness.)

* Add sugar (27 ounces for Fleischmann's yeast, 35
   ounces for wine yeast).
* Add water to fill $^3/_4$ of the way up.
* Add yeast. Stir.
* When initial foaming subsides, top up with water.
* Ferment.
* Decant. Set in a cool place to settle out.

GROCERY STORE WINE

An insipid wine, but foolproof. Good for beginners to start
with, for confidence.
* Put 19 ounces white sugar into a 1-gallon jug.
* Add a large can of Welch's frozen Concord grape
   concentrate.
* Add water to fill $^3/_4$ of the jug. Stir.
* Add one package Fleischmann's dry yeast.
* When initial foaming has subsided, top up with water.
* Ferment.
* Settle out.
Being bland, this product lends itself well to freeze-
   concentrating.

Now that you know how to make all these good products, I hope
you put the knowledge to good use. "I'll drink to that!" you're supposed to answer.

One last word on the subject: *Don't drink and drive*! You have the right to commit suicide if you want, but you do *not* have the right to kill or mangle innocent people, which is what drunken drivers eventually do. We live near a dangerous intersection, and I could tell you some stories—horror stories—about drunken drivers.

13.
Housing

Housing is what makes it or breaks it for possum living. If you're renting or paying off a mortgage, you are locked into the money economy, period. End of sentence.

Diogenes solved the problem with his barrel, but if you try it around here you will get not only frostbite but an unpleasant visit from the zoning officer as well.

Owning your own home free and clear—that's the key to all the rest. Once you have your snug harbor, your safe base, all else comes easy. You can tell the rest of the world to go to hell if you want, once you own the roof over your head. I believe that some parents who are willing to scrimp and save to give their kid a college education would be doing the kid a better turn by giving him that money to buy a house instead. Once he realizes he doesn't have to worry about his future—once he has security and leisure to think about it, instead of having his future rammed down his throat—he'll make his own future.

I had thought to point up some fallacies of the notion of housing as a bona fide investment, but now I think better of it. You can make money in real estate, true, but the ordinary homeowner paying off a mortgage is not really investing. If you have possum instincts I don't have to tell you this, and if you don't I won't convince you. True possums, read on—others, do what you will.

Inexpensive and adequate housing in desirable areas actually does exist, believe it or not. (No, I *don't* still leave out carrots for the Easter Bunny, either!) It exists, but it's hard, hard, hard to find. But then so is paying off a twenty-year mortgage hard.

Most people are on a sort of treadmill which allows them neither the leisure nor the cash to look around and evaluate their housing opportunities and requirements. They need a house near their job, so they can get to their job, and they need the job to pay for the house. This is something of a vicious circle.

It really doesn't take much money by today's standards (our home cost us $6,100 in 1974—less than a year's income for the average family!), but it does require that the wealth be in the form of cash. Assets are great, but cash is what gets the job done. To get the cash, you might resort to miserism.

Previously I promised not to proselytize miserism, but now I want to renege a little on that promise. If your family income is anywhere near average, you can scrimp and save and cut back for maybe two to four years and save up the capital to become free for the rest of your life. And give your children a heritage of freedom besides, which is the main thing. Either it's worth it to you or it isn't.

Have you read John Steinbeck's *The Grapes of Wrath*? When we read it, it completely amazed us. All that starvation, squalor, and general misery the Okies were forced to endure stemmed from only two roots: (1) the fact that they didn't own their homes outright, and (2) their mule-headed determination to rely on the money economy. They would have had problems, but not all the grief they had, if they had owned their homesteads in Oklahoma. The geek who stayed behind living on wild rabbits probably wound up living better than anyone else in the story.

I don't mean to imply that a 1929-type economic debacle is going to reoccur, but the thought of it does prey on many people's minds. Others—not us—swear we're now entering the age of shortages. If true, it wouldn't affect us homeowning possums much one way or t'other.

✳ Low-Cost Housing ✳

In some big cities they're practically giving away housing in the neighborhoods that are no longer fit to live in. The phrase "no longer fit to live in" covers this situation adequately and no more need be said.

In some parts of the country you can still build your own home the way you want it built, but in the more populated areas zoning regulations are such that it'll cost you about as much to build as to buy. The exceptions are in the more dreary sections of the boondocks, where no one wants to live.

Trailers are a possibility, and we have lived in them in Florida. But again, you have zoning and squalor problems, not to mention limited space.

That leaves finding and buying cheap housing. It isn't easy, and it isn't fast. However, it is easier and faster than paying off a twenty-year mortgage.

Just a few examples: Near us a grain elevator was bought and occupied at a cost of $6,000 in 1968. It's made of stone and is very solid. The people living there have fixed up the top part as a penthouse and the bottom as a garage and storage area. We ourselves almost paid $9,000 for a very a substantial stone-walled church sitting on a one-acre lot adjacent to *very* quiet neighbors. There are many outmoded schoolhouses in our area that people are living in, and I can't imagine they paid very much for them. We once rented a barn and lived in it for four months, and we see other people living in renovated barns.

Zoning laws may prohibit the use of churches, grain elevators, etc. as habitations. But the zoning people don't usually go looking for trouble. If you are quiet, unobtrusive, and pleasant to the neighbors, and don't introduce any innovations into the neighborhood—in other words, if you give the neighbors reason to believe you'll be a good neighbor—you needn't expect any difficulties. If, on the other hand, you're determined to stand on your rights, they'll harass you till you feel like leaving. They can and they will.

In the case of the church we were considering buying, we

intended to simply deny we were living there if anyone should ask. We were going to list my uncle's place as our official residence. They would have had to take us to court to prove otherwise, despite how obvious it may have been, and it just doesn't seem likely anyone would go to all that trouble. If any neighbor, out of perverseness, had insisted on his zoning rights, we would have simply gone and reasoned with him. Of course, if you have kids that you want to put in the local public school, you might have a problem. Once you have established yourself for a year or two, it shouldn't be hard to get a zoning exception.

You could try riding around looking for abandoned houses. When you find one, look up the owner's name on the maps in the tax assessment office. Then look up the deed (if you don't know how, I'll explain later) to see how much the owner paid for it (you should do this with every property you want to buy). Make an offer to the owner. If the house looks like a rat trap (which it probably will), don't be deterred. Imagine what it will look like fixed up, cleaned, and painted, with the lawn mowed, etc.

If you don't want to or can't buy it, perhaps the owner would be willing to give you a long-term lease at low rates in exchange for your fixing it up. A friend of ours made just such a deal.

Or you could go, as we did, to sheriff sales. We did, in fact, buy our present house at a foreclosure sale. It wasn't easy, and it took us two years of work. In fact, it was very discouraging. You don't normally get bargains at sheriff sales, despite what you may have read. If the property's at all desirable, speculators will be in on the action. We finally got our place only because of an economic fluke: Mortgage money became totally unavailable for a short time and the speculators held off buying because they couldn't quickly unload. Normally a speculator can afford to bid higher than you on a given property due to certain idiotic tax regulations concerning low-cost housing.

Two or three weeks before the monthly sale, the sheriff will put up handbills on the walls of his office at the county courthouse describing the properties to be sold. Foreclosure sale details vary from state to state and even from county to county. *Warning*: Even some lawyers don't know what they're doing, so *don't rely on advice from inexperienced persons*. Many people apparently are unaware that all debts are *not* automatically canceled by a foreclosure proceeding.

I'm going to tell you about Montgomery County, Pa., as an example. You'll have to find out on your own the fine details of other jurisdictions. I don't know about, nor could I possibly list, all the counties in the nation, of course.

* How Foreclosure Sales Work *

Two weeks or so before the sale, go to the sheriff's office and pick up the handbill on any property of interest.

The writ of execution will be filed at the county prothonotary's office. Give the clerk the number listed on the handbill and ask to see it. It describes the action of the common pleas court in foreclosing on the property.

Write down:
* The defendants' exact names, initials included. (Most often it will be a jointly owned husband/wife property. Get both names.)
* The plaintiff's name. (Usually a bank.)
* The plaintiff's attorney's name. (The attorney-on-the-writ. You might want to talk to him later.)

Verify the following:
* An affidavit must be included showing that neither defendant was a member of the U.S. armed forces at the time the debt was contracted.
* The debt must have been contracted by both parties of a jointly owned property. ("Jointly and severally" is the usual phrase.)
* An attempt was made to locate and serve notice to both parties.

Next, go to the tax assessor's office (map room). There you will find books on each township and borough in the county. Each book has the streets listed in alphabetical order. Look in the appropriate place till you find the names of the defendants. Check that the names exactly match those on the writ—if you find, say, two or three J. Joneses in one neighborhood, you had better be sure you have the right J. Jones. It occasionally happens that townships change street names and you can't find what you want. You then must scan through the whole book. When you

find your place, write down:
* the tax assessment
* the block and unit number (Example: B63-U16)
* deed number
* deed date

(If the deed information isn't available, you can look it up later.)

In the same office you find map books showing the physical location of the block-and-unit listed properties. Copy out a little map so you can go and inspect the property. (Theoretically, it's illegal to enter the place, even if it's abandoned, but we always did when we could.)

Go to the office of the recorder of deeds and look up the deed. If you didn't get the number, you must look it up in the "grantee" books. These and others are usually arranged by the dates of the entries made in them, and by the initials of the surnames of the parties entered. On the inside cover of each book you'll find the "key system" of references explained. There's a "key number" for any name, and you look in that section of the book for the information you want. It's complicated, but you can get one of the clerks to help you. The clerks are public employees and are happy to assist polite citizens. In fact, if you look puzzled, they'll generally approach you and offer to help. When you get the copy of the deed, check that

* The owners' names and the description of the property match those found on the writ.

* You have the correct deed date.
* See if a land title company put its mark on the back.
* Write down the previous owners' names in case you decide to search the title back further.

Next, look up the parties' names in the "grantor" books to make sure they didn't manage to sell off the place before they got foreclosed. You need search back only as far as the deed date, of course.

Now you know the defendants really do own the place—they did buy it and they didn't sell it. You also know they're being legally foreclosed. It only remains for you to find out if any debts remain to be paid once you've bought the place from the sheriff.

You needn't concern yourself with any debts that were *registered* after the foreclosing debt was registered—they are canceled by the foreclosure sale. It doesn't matter if they're mortgages or money judgments, or when they were contracted. The registration date is the only consideration of whether or not they remain in effect against the property.

Debts registered prior to the foreclosing debt remain in effect and must be paid, or they could result in a foreclosure action against you at a later time.

You find out about mortgages by searching the mortgage books, also located in the office of the recorder of deeds. Money judgments are registered in the Judgment Index located in the prothonotary's office. Money judgments remain in effect for only five years (unless reregistered), so you don't have to search back further than that. If you find anything, check that it's registered against both parties of a jointly owned property—if it isn't, ignore it.

We've never encountered the situation, but it's theoretically possible for debts registered against a previous owner to remain valid against a property even after it's been legally sold. If a land title company insured it, or if a bank or mortgage company lent mortgage money on it at the time of the sale (check the dates), it was almost certainly clear at that time, but otherwise you might better search back to the previous owner's records. Remember: A mortgage sticks till it's either paid or canceled by a foreclosure action, and the only way a money judgment differs, for practical considerations, is in its five-year expiration date. When debts are satisfied, an "S" is marked on the record.

Property taxes are paid up to date by the sheriff, so you needn't worry about that. He also pays the transfer tax, so the only closing cost is $35, or something like that, to have the deed registered.

Following is a sample of the form we used to keep the information orderly:

Sheriff's handbill ...... (1)   Writ number _____

Writ of execution ...... (2)   Defendants' names _____ & _____

(3)   Plaintiff_____

(4)   Attorney-on-the-writ_____

(5)   Cost & debt _____

(6)   Armed Forces?   [ ] yes [ ] no

(7)   Notice attempted to defendants?
                        [ ] yes [ ] no

(8)   Township—address_____

Tax Assessor's office... (9)   Block & Unit_____

(10) Assessment_____

(11) Deed # _____

(12) Deed date _____

(13) Remember to draw map.

Recorder of Deeds .... (14)   Defendants' "key numbers" __ & __

(15) Grantor book clear? [ ] yes [ ] no

(16) Deed info. correct?   [ ] yes [ ] no

(17) Sale price $_____

(18) Mortgages_____
            date - amount - lender

            _____
            date - amount - lender

Prothonotary's office.. (19)   Judgments_____
            date - amount - lender

            _____
            date - amount - lender

Other................. (20)   Estimated value $_____

(21) Remaining debts $_____

(22) Top bid I will make $_____

If debts will remain after the sale, you can't make an intelligent bid until you know how much of them remains unpaid. The easiest way to find out is to simply call up the creditors and ask them. Tell them you're searching titles for someone else—they're more likely to help out a working stiff than a speculator. If you can't find out, you can only proceed on the assumption that none of it has been paid. In the case of mortgages held by big companies, you can gamble that the payments are fairly up to date (or *they* would have foreclosed), but it is a gamble.

How much to bid? Only you know what the place is worth to you. Some people use the tax assessment and last sale price as guides, but they are only rough measurements. It might be wise to look up a few places and attend a few sales before venturing to bid, so you get a feel for it. In any case, never bid more than the cash you have available—the sheriff wants 10% in green money immediately and the balance in 20 days. If you can't come up with the balance, you forfeit the down payment money, so don't count on getting a loan to pay it unless you *really* like to gamble.

Remember to hold back enough to pay off prior debts, and to fix the place up if it isn't fit to live in. (Of course, once it's liveable, you can make other repairs at your leisure.)

Once you pay the full sum, the sheriff will make out a deed and record it. You then own that property same as if you bought it on the open market.

If the speculators consistently outbid you, you might try this: Go to all the sales and bid and bid. After getting beat out by the obvious speculators a few times, approach them after the sale and explain that you aren't speculating, you are merely looking for a homestead. Explain that once you have your property you will no longer bid on other properties. Point out that every time you bid up property it's costing them money to overbid you. Explain that it would be good business on their part to let one fall to you just to be rid of you. It might work, depending on how well you talk.

It occasionally happens that a property will be foreclosed and the total of the debt and costs will be higher than the actual market value of the place. (Either the owner was a good talker or the place sustained fire or other damage.) Get in touch with the attorney handling the foreclosure writ and tell him what you think the place is worth and what you will bid, and ask him to consider forgoing the normal practice of bidding up to the cost and debt value. In other words, explain that they might as well "bite the bullet" at the sale as later, when they go to unload it. They will at least save handling costs that way, you point out.

At least once in our experience the principal creditor actually put up a For Sale sign and obtained an agreement of sale on an abandoned property before it had been "knocked down" by the sheriff. This was in Lehigh County, Pa. If this happens where you are trying to buy, get in touch with the realtor handling the sale and put up a beef. It's illegal in Pennsylvania, as in other states, to sell a property you don't own, and the registered party owns it till the time the sheriff bangs the gavel. Daddy settled their hash by bidding just under the sale price, so they didn't make any profit on the deal. He could have (and should have) filed a complaint with the state real-estate commission, which would probably have forestalled any recurrence of the practice in that area for at least a short time.

* Back-Tax Sales *

Frankly, I don't know much about this subject. These sales are held only once a year and draw so many speculators it never seemed like a worthwhile project to us. I'm sure if you go to your county tax office you can get an explanation of the procedure, since the more bidders present the more likely the tax office is to collect its money.

There is another procedure that I have read about but of which I have no first-hand knowledge. You get a list of delinquent taxes due on properties from the county authorities and pick out a property you would like to own. Then you pay up the back taxes and keep them paid for a given number of years (usually two). If the owner doesn't settle up by then, you acquire title to the place. I don't know if registered debts remain to be paid or are canceled with this method, but I would guess they'd stand. It would seem very likely that you'd have your money tied up and then either the owner would pay up at the last minute, or some creditor would foreclose and set you back on "square one."

* Home Repairs *

In many townships, you're supposed to get a building permit before making repairs on a property. If you're a law-and-order fanatic, go ahead, but we never have. It's just asking for some jack-in-the-office to come stick his nose into your business. We once plastered over the entire outside of a three-story building in a suburban neighborhood—a $2,000 job—without a permit, and no one said a word about it.

When we bought our house it wasn't fit to live in. The pipes and the toilet were busted from freezing. There wasn't any bathroom proper (the house having previously been a country store). Bricks were crumbling and falling out of the wall. There was a doorway leading out with no door and no steps. The cellar floor was mud. There were broken windows. The place was full of junk and rats. There were no heating facilities on the second floor. The porch and cellarway were cracked and tumbling. The wiring was faulty. The lot was just junk and weeds, right up to the doors. And to top it all, a huge poison ivy vine had grown up the wall and was forcing tendrils under the window. But what do you expect for $6,100?

Looking back, I can scarce believe it, but we corrected all those faults and more besides in less than a year. We got some help with the carpentry from Daddy's uncle, but the plumbing, electrical work, concrete and masonry work, and landscaping were done mostly by Daddy and me. We had no prior experience in any related fields, either. We acquired a complete set of do-it-yourself books, read up carefully on each subject, and just jumped in with two feet and got the job done. Sure we made mistakes, but so what? We learned from them, corrected them, and went on. Now the job is done and the money we would have spent to have someone else do it is still in the bank. And we learned how to do the work—I could now earn money doing this work if I wanted to.

Work you do on your own home is better than money, since you needn't pay income tax on it. That isn't the main consideration, though. Mainly, it's pleasant and satisfying to live in a house that became a home by the fruits of your own labor.

* Your Property Tax Assessment *

Before you make extensive repairs on the tumbledown hobo shack you bought (get used to using those kinds of terms), go to the tax assessor's office and cry on his shoulder. Chances are the assessment was made before the place became dilapidated, and you might get it lowered. Compare your assessment with those of others in your neighborhood against their last sale prices. (One property here sold for five times what ours went for, and yet had a lower assessment. Daddy made sure the tax people knew ours should be lowered!) A zoning change from commercial to residential, as in the cases of the grain elevator and our country store, also lowers the value of a property, which should be reflected in the assessment. In Pennsylvania, at least, the law states that the assessment must be based on the actual market value of the property. If the tax people won't be reasonable at first, talk about legal action—they don't want to go to court any more than you do.

14.
Heating

We use an oil burner because it came with the house, but we intend to phase it out in another year or two. We've already installed a wood burner in the kitchen. We didn't buy it, of course, we made it. (See illustration.) Frankly, it's inefficiently designed, but its use has nevertheless cut our oil consumption by about half. The stovepipe, damper, and plywood were purchased (about $15), and the drum and other parts we got at a dump. To get the stovepipe outside, we simply removed a window and replaced it with a sheet of plywood. In this we cut a large hole and nailed on a piece of sheet metal. The stovepipe goes through a hole in the sheet metal. It works almost as well as a storebought model, and the thought of the extra $200 or so we saved on the purchase price also helps keep us warm. One big advantage of this stove is that we can put a cookie sheet on top with water in it and restore

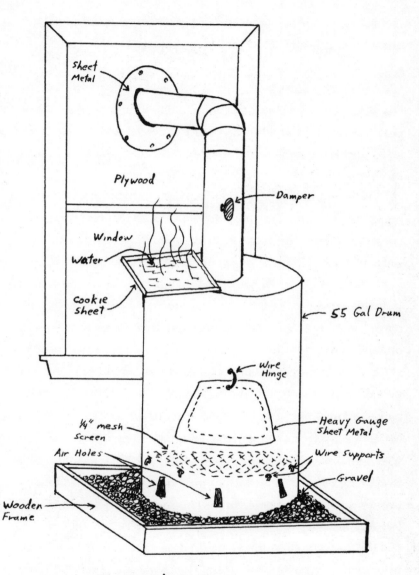

Our Wood-Burner

moisture to the air. Some heating systems dry out the air till the humidity is literally below that of the Sahara Desert.

We have no problem getting fuel. A local store throws out cardboard and wooden shipping crates, neighbors give us stacks of old newspapers, and there are plenty of dead branches and trees and a few old tumbledown wooden buildings here. We have a two-person saw and an ax for cutting the wood.

We've studied up on solar heating (your library will have books on this subject) and plan to build a unit, probably next summer. We are fortunate in having an almost blank wall facing south. We will paint this wall flat black, then build a system of copper pipes against the wall, and enclose it with glass held in wooden frames. This will be connected, through electrically controlled valves (zone boxes, thermostatically controlled), with our existing hot-water system.

Unfortunately, this old house has little insulation and can't be easily insulated. In fact, we despaired of heating the upper story and now we close it off and don't use it in the winter. We bring our mattresses down and sleep Japanese style on the living room floor. Then, too, we insulated and sealed off four of the five living room windows that we didn't use, and that helped immensely. It's also cooler in the summer from that, and we get less traffic noise.

We keep the thermostat at 60°F (we were wearing sweaters indoors before anyone outside of Georgia even heard of Jimmy Carter), and we turn off the oil furnace at night. We also turn it off when we go out for any length of time. In warm weather we keep it off except when we want to bathe or wash dishes (we have a summer-winter hookup). Since the electrical switch controlling the furnace is mounted on a beam right under the floorboards, we drilled a small hole in the floor and use an ice-pick to flick the switch on and off. If your furnace switch isn't so conveniently mounted it shouldn't be much trouble to relocate it if you want to have this same convenient control.

I've read a consumer magazine that said it might not pay to turn off the heat at night because you use more fuel getting the place warm again in the morning. That's absurd, of course. Maybe someone should do a consumer report on the quality of consumer magazines. The BTUs lost through the walls is proportional to the temperature differential between the inside and outside. Keeping the inside warm at night means more BTUs lost, and therefore to be replaced. You replace them by burning fuel. When you turn off the heat, the inside temperature falls at an exponential rate (assuming the outside temperature to be constant), which means that the rate of BTU loss is constantly going down as the inside temperature goes down, and the temperature goes down with the accumulated loss of BTUs. (Equations supplied on demand.) So turn the god-damn thing off at night and save yourself some money.

15.
Electricity

Electricity is a real bargain when you consider what you get for your money. Nevertheless, you do well to keep in mind that it isn't essential for human life. The general use of electricity didn't come about until the end of the 19th century, and millions upon millions of happy, healthy people lived satisfying lives without it. In our area many Amish people, some of them quite prosperous, still eschew it on religious grounds.

We use about 230 kilowatt-hours per bimonthly period, which costs us $16. Our water pump and the pumps on the oil burner are the big users, and we haven't yet figured a way around using them. The refrigerator doesn't take much (we insulated its door well with foam rubber), and when we don't have perishables on hand we turn it off. In cold weather we keep the perishables on the stairway and thus avoid using it then, too. Of course, it's not automatic defrost. We do use light bulbs and also indulge ourselves with a radio and a clock.

Aside from the money aspect, we also conscientiously use as little electricity as possible because "increasing demand" is the justification for building nuclear power plants. That controversy is outside the scope of this book and I'm not going to go into it further than to point out that anyone who is opposed to nuclear power and yet uses an electric dishwasher, clothes dryer, air conditioner, TV, or any of the other toys people have been conned into thinking they need, is no better than the power company executives who think they need atomic power plants for toys.

We will probably, at some future date, buy or build wind-powered generating equipment, but not yet. The technology is still improving and the prices are still coming down, so we feel it's better to wait awhile yet.

16.
Clothing

The implementation of buying prestige and status is often through the medium of clothing. I hate to say it, but this seems to be especially true of women.

Once when Daddy worked for Manpower he had a two-week job working for a business that sold fashionable women's clothing. Ladies would come in—all sorts of ladies, from all sorts of backgrounds, usually with several friends—and start buying (on time payments, naturally). The distinct impression was that they didn't have as much need for clothing as they had to impress their friends and the saleslady with the size of the bundle they were dropping. Then, right out in public, they'd agree among themselves on what lies they would tell their husbands regarding the cost of the various items.

I completely fail to understand this mentality. No doubt

they would fail to understand us, so that makes us even.

We get all our clothing at the thrift shop. We're fortunate in that our local church thrift shop is extremely reasonable (there are thrift shops and there are thrift shops). Daddy's entire wardrobe, excluding running shoes, cost about $10. Mine, also excluding running shoes, cost about $15.

Well, I know what you're thinking: I'm some poor, dowdy little thing and Daddy looks like the scarecrow from *The Wizard of Oz*. Now, how can I say this without seeming immodest? The truth is that when I get dressed up I'm a knockout. I go out on dates and no one seems ashamed to be seen with me. And while Daddy usually does look like a scarecrow, he, too, is presentable when he wants to be.

Okay, you say, how does all this fine clothing wind up in a thrift shop? That's easily answered: The ladies who need to show off their spending power also need to make room in their closets before they can buy new clothes. Then, too, many people go on diets and lose weight, treat themselves to a whole new wardrobe to celebrate, and then gain the weight back and have no use for the clothes.

I have a sewing machine that I never use. It's cheaper to buy clothing at the thrift shop than to buy the patterns and cloth to make them.

Children's clothing is even more plentiful at thrift shops because, of course, children quickly outgrow their clothes.

17.
Transportation

In our society the automobile is many things to many people. To the suburbanite it has become what the horse was to the Plains Indians—the whole basis of the culture. To a great many men and boys it's the premier status symbol. Daddy says that when he was a young man the guys would do almost anything to get "wheels," because the girls wouldn't even look at you otherwise, and hormones win out over common sense every time. Environmentalists see the automobile, both in its manufacture and operation, as the main ingredient of our monumental pollution problem.

We haven't had a car for three years now, and there has been some inconvenience because of it. But then there's an awful lot of inconvenience to owning a car, too: insurance, maintenance, gas worry, traffic jams, parking—and mainly money. Freedom of mobility doesn't come cheap.

Unfortunately, there's virtually zero public transportation in our area, so we walk, run, or bicycle everywhere we go. There's a little town 2 miles from our house, and when we need anything— groceries, hardware, etc.—we walk there pulling a grocery cart (the geek-mobile). We do quite a bit of walking and cycling. It doesn't seem to have harmed us. In fact, we enjoy it. Walking or cycling, you really do notice a lot more about the things going on around you than you do from a speeding car, trite as that may sound.

A word or two about our chief mode of transportation: A good three-speed bike is better than a ten-speed bike for practical transportation purposes. It's easier to ride, easier to maintain, less a target for thieves, and less expensive then a ten-speed. We bought our bikes at yard sales rather than from dealers. However, don't look for a terrific bargain, because if you get one you'll be buying stolen merchandise. Don't encourage thieving—your bike might be the next to disappear.

Our main problem is getting heavy bags from the grain store. We have friends with whom we exchange various favors, and who keep animals, so they help us out with that. Sometimes the store will deliver.

For a while we had the use of a horse without the expense or bother of owning one. It turns out that many people want to own horses but have no place to keep them, so they "board them out." A neighbor here was keeping one of these horses in his barn and since he wanted it to get exercise, he let us use it whenever we wanted. (Once we got it in good shape, though, he sold it on us!)

Now we're thinking of building a two-horse stable (it shouldn't cost more than about $500 if we do the labor) and boarding horses. The boarding fees would cover the expenses in a year or two; we'd have the use of the animals for transportation, and the extra manure for the garden.

18.
Law

From my admittedly limited experience I would have to guess that Americans of my social stratum don't put much stock in government and law. I don't think I know an adult man who doesn't own a gun—"just in case." Nor do any people I know pay any taxes they can possibly avoid.

Despite all the idiots and greedy swine in our government, we do have a pretty good system, I think. I own a paperback book, *The Rights You Have*, by Osmond K. Fraenkel, that spells out the constitutional rights of American citizens. You owe it to yourself to learn what your rights are, and to insist that they not be violated.

Everyday nitty-gritty law is more in line with the purpose of this book, because lawyers can really cost you big money. (Moneyers would be a more appropriate term for some of them.) Before hiring a lawyer, think it over. Do you really need one? What can he do for you that you can't do for yourself? Think about money. If you're honest and fair, and know how to speak English, you should never need a lawyer. A society that requires honest people to hire other people to speak or write for them when they want to reach an agreement with others is a flawed society, I think. If you do decide to hire a lawyer, insist on a cost estimate. Don't be afraid to shop around—there are plenty of lawyers.

There have been times when it seemed we just couldn't do without a lawyer, but we always did. So might you.

Once, when we were still in the money economy, a cutey-pie of a realtor got hold of several thousand of ours by sheer fraud and wouldn't give it back. He spouted fountains of legal technicalities.

Daddy assured us that a man—any man—is a reasoning creature and can be reasoned with. "He knows he's being dishonest and so I'll just reason with him," said Daddy. "First, though, I may have to catch his attention."

So Daddy looked up his address at the county Recorder of Deeds office, then visited his house late one night and caught his attention. Sure enough, once the realtor's attention was caught he realized his rotten ways were wrong and returned the money. Even paid interest on it.

When Mom was getting the divorce, Daddy went to talk to her lawyer about making a settlement with her. It soon became obvious, however, that the lawyer had no intention of effecting a quick settlement. The longer he could drag out the agony the more fees he could collect. Isn't it disgusting what people will do for money?

Well, Daddy knew this precious lamb wasn't going to be reasonable about it until his attention was caught and he realized how serious this was to us, so Daddy visited his house that night and caught his attention. And what do you think? That lawyer was a reasonable man after all and dropped the case like a hot potato. Then Mom hired a decent lawyer and they settled up like two civilized human beings. Daddy never did hire a lawyer.

Now, I'm perfectly aware that some people might think these methods reprehensible—I myself am appalled at the incidences of senseless terrorism so common today. I am *not* advocating terrorism, however. I wasn't being sarcastic or "cute" when I said what I did about catching your adversary's attention and then reasoning with him (or causing him to reason with himself, rather). That really is what happens. What you must keep in mind is that many people, out of greed, have convinced themselves that it's okay for them to do whatever they want so long as it's strictly legal. But we don't want law for the sake of law, we want it for the sake of justice—and often don't get it. That realtor and that lawyer may have won out if we had played the game according to their rules—the legal code—but there wouldn't have been any justice involved. So we didn't play by their rules. Daddy made up his own. Here they are:

* Rules *

* Be sure you're right and your adversary is wrong. *These methods work only on people having a guilty conscience.*

* Keep your goal clearly in mind. The goal is to get your money back, or get the guy to stop hassling you, or whatever. The goal is not revenge or an ego trip, or an excuse to vent your spleen.

* Go only so far as is necessary to attain the goal. Give him a chance to do the right thing. His guilty conscience is your best ally, but if you overdo it right off the bat, before he has a chance to reevaluate his position, his guilt feelings will be replaced by outrage, and the situation could get out of hand.

You must proceed *intelligently*. If you can't control your temper, you're going to blow the game. A friend of ours—a hot-tempered man—lost his cool and threatened his wife's lawyer in open court. He not only lost the suit, he also spent thirty days in jail for contempt of court and making threats.

* Procedure *

* If possible, call your adversary on the phone during normal business hours. Calmly and dispassionately explain your position. Don't threaten him.

*Give him a reasonable length of time to think over his position.

*Call him again—preferably late at night—and curse and threaten him. Do not identify yourself or refer to anything that you alone might know. (He'll recognize your voice from the other call, but won't be able to prove it.) Do not repeat the call—once is enough for your purpose. Do not specifically say when or where the trouble he is in for is going to occur. If ever accused of this call, deny it.

Now comes the hard part—you have to convince him he's vulnerable.

* Visit his house late at night and do something to let him know he has an enemy who has no intention of playing the game by his rules. (If you don't know his address, look it up at the courthouse. I explained how on page 155.) Do *not* take a weapon or anything that could be called a weapon that you wouldn't want to discard if necessary. Go on foot. I'm going to leave it to your imagination as to what to do when you get there. However, some people say that houses have windows, and others have it that bricks may be found. And cars are often left out at night and might have their tires about them at such times. And still others say telephone lines run outside of houses and are thin. And I've heard that penknives are sharp. Don't be in a

179

hurry—look the situation over for potential. Perhaps he has a dog, so you might want to take along some liver or meat to befriend it. If the dog is downright vicious, come back another time and poison it. It's no sin to kill a vicious animal, and it will make your adversary feel more vulnerable.

* It's perfectly legal for you to knock on his door because you want to talk over the difficulty, as long as you don't use threatening or abusive terms or he hasn't sworn out a peace bond on the matter. (Don't show anger under any circumstances—better act simple.) The mere knowledge that you are concerned enough to go to so much trouble (and know where to get him) might be enough to give him pause to reevaluate his position. Let's hope so, so you don't have to come back another time, and also to save him trouble. If he orders you to leave, do so immediately—your mere appearance has accomplished your purpose. If the cops show up, dispassionately explain that you were upset and merely wanted to discuss the matter. Remember—you're simple. Don't show any emotion except perhaps despair—the cops are human and will merely wish to be rid of you, if you only give them the chance. If you don't seem threatening (which you won't, by design), you'll simply be dismissed.

* Make no further contact with him for a while. He'll be hyped up from the adrenalin discharge caused by

the incident. In three days this will wear off, leaving him depressed and fair game for his guilty conscience. Then, too, his family will want to know what's going on. His greed may override his guilt, but he may still be ashamed to let his loved ones know what a rat he is. Don't have scruples about getting his family involved— they *do* get the material benefits of his sordid dealings, you know. Let them know at what price in infamy they get their luxury.

*If he doesn't come around on his own, about four days after the incident call him during business hours and talk over the situation. Don't gloat. Don't admit or hint around that you did anything. Let him save face and chances are he'll let you talk him into taking a fairer stance. If he doesn't—go back to the third step.

You may not want to do all this. You may not be equipped to handle the adrenalin discharges involved. Or you may have ethical reservations. Those are two legitimate points. However, in many of these stressful legal hassles you're going to get your adrenalin stirred up one way or another, anyhow, so you might as well choose your own time and place rather than have the clerk of court appoint it for you. After all, who's managing your adrenalin discharges, you or some lousy clerk of court? And ethics boils down to justice—you're either just or unjust. If you're satisfied you're right—what do you care what some judge or other person thinks?

It's harmful to your health to have a worry hanging over your head for any length of time if you happen to be a certain physiological type of person. You need it to be settled. Cut the gordian knot! Our legal system is probably the best ever designed for the overall population it serves, but that fact is small consolation to us hyper-adrenalin citizens. The "law's delays" have been criticized at least since Shakespeare's time and are still a point of contention today. As Diogenes recognized, 2,300 years ago, "justice is what all rational people want, and law is the substitute they are sometimes willing to accept." The best course is to avoid situations likely to lead to legal action, but failing that, settling out of court is the next best. But do it yourself.

Older and wiser, I no longer agree with what I wrote in this chapter.

—Dolly Freed, 2009

19.
Health and
Medicine

Despite the problems facing the world today, I'm still glad I live now instead of in the "good old days." Medical science has freed me of that long list of horrendous diseases that were so much a part of life in those good old days, and I'm grateful. Of course, there's a price tag.

It reads $547 annually for every man, woman, and child in America. According to the president of Blue Cross, that's what the average American spends on health care each year (but then, of course, this guy *does* sell health insurance). It totals up to $118 billion—10% of the GNP (1975 figures). I've read that it's likely to be double that by 1980.

However, these figures are somewhat misleading since they

include such things as cosmetic plastic surgery, various vague therapies, dental braces, and other nonessential medical care. Then again it's not unheard of for thousands of dollars to be spent on heroic efforts to extend the life of some poor ancient geezer for a few more months.

These things, of course, contribute to the total and thereby increase the average. I would be interested in seeing the figures on strictly essential care for normal, basically healthy people. My guess would be that it would be something in the order of $20 a year (1976 dollars) over the person's lifetime.

We don't spend any. None. Zero expenditure. No annual checkup, no insurance, no therapy, no dental care (although Daddy did have a tooth pulled about two years ago).

Daddy had his tonsils removed to cure poison ivy when he was 10 and has been mad at doctors ever since. His knee used to painfully and mysteriously swell up every so often, and the quack said it was from toxins generated by infected tonsils, and took them out. Later on, Daddy noticed that every time he recovered from poison ivy, three days later the knee would swell. Well, when he was 10 he was always getting poison ivy, which no doubt was the cause then, too.

He did get a shot of penicillin when he had pneumonia, and I got some stitches for a cut forehead once, and that's about it in recent years.

People always ask what would we do if we were to get seriously ill, and we always answer, truthfully, "I dunno." This seems to bug people no end, for some reason, so I guess we're going to have to come up with something better to say. (We aren't argumentative at all.)

We could say, "Trust in the care of the Lord," I guess, but then people who know us know we aren't that religious. Or maybe, "If I'm that sick I'd rather End It All than be an invalid." But that, while easy to say while one is healthy and the sun is shining, may not be true. Who knows till it happens? Probably, "I'd rather be sick than shell out $547 per year" would be closest to the truth.

We like Plato's opinion on the subject. He said, "When a working man is ill he asks the physician for a rough and ready remedy—an emetic, or a purge, or cautery, or the knife. And if anyone tells him that he must go through a course of dietetics, and swathe and swaddle his head, and all that sort of thing, he replies at once that he has no time to be ill, and that he sees no good in a life that is spent in nursing his disease to the neglect of his ordinary calling, and therefore, saying good-bye to this sort of physician, he resumes his customary diet, and either gets well and lives and does his business, or, if his constitution fails, he dies and has done with it."

Let's grope our way out of this murky den. The first aspect of health is to have a healthy mind—a healthy outlook on life. If you have to go through life worrying about getting sick, what's the sense of it? Maybe those ostriches that stick their heads in the sand aren't so dumb after all—at least they don't get ulcers from worry.

Let me tell you about a man I once met. I don't even remember his name, but I really admire him. He knew he had a congenital heart condition and a life expectancy of about 45 years if he took care of himself. So he joined a running club and died on a street in Philadelphia, still in his thirties, while running a 9-mile race. That's the kind of courage to have! He died like a man, in an athletic contest, rather than live an invalid's life and slowly sputter out in some bleak hospital. What a Viking he would have made! And what a reproach his example should be to all the timid ninnies who are so concerned with health insurance and medical programs.

Probably the main reason we don't worry about health is that we feel healthy. We eat well. (We laughed and laughed when that "high fiber content" diet fad came out. We had been eating that way for years, out of preference.) And we also get exercise aplenty, again by preference, not as a conscious health aid. Please note that "exercise" and "work" are two entirely different things. They even have some exact opposite physiological effects. This distinction is often ignored.

We run. No, we don't jog. Jogging is a dull, boring, futile pastime. The proof of that last statement is that of the vast horde of joggers spawned by the fad of a few years ago, about 99% are back in front of the boob tube with a beer can in their hand. Joggers quit—runners don't. There are men in their sixties and seventies still competing in age group races. Although jogging has merit as a conditioner and warm-up for running, a steady diet of it can be depressing.

Running, on the other hand, is exciting—a form of socially acceptable violence. When you feel that adrenalin surging through your veins, you know what it means to be alive! When you recover from a good work-out, you feel clean. Weight-lifters and rowers say the same thing about their exertions.

Daddy tried to give up running once and found himself getting moody, gloomy, irritable, and having thoughts of sickness, purposelessness, futility, and death on his mind all the time. He could have tried transcendental meditation or patronized one of those two-bit gurus who abound lately, or found Jesus, or bought health insurance, but he didn't. He simply went back to running.

* Dolly's Depression Dispersing Directions *

(1) (For healthy males 16–40) Jog 2–5 miles three to five days per week for at least four weeks, for conditioning. Don't do more. Don't push the pace. Be restrained.

(2) Rest two days.

(3) Run 2 miles as hard as you can, two hours after eating a regular meal. Drink all the hot, sweet tea you can before running. The run should hurt.

(4) Rest, bundled up, in a warm place two hours. Drink hot, sweet tea. Do stretching exercises. Sweat. Crap.

(5) Jog slowly fifteen minutes. Walk five minutes. Think heroic thoughts.

(6) Run till your heart feels like it will burst your ribs. Run till your eyeballs pop out. Run till your lungs gasp for air. Run till it feels like your intestines are being twisted by a giant hand. Run till you can't stand it. Run till you

have to slow down, then run faster. Run till you can go no farther—then go farther. Plan for about 5 miles.

(7) Run easier five days per week, for two weeks. Then repeat the five previous steps. Go for quality rather than quantity on your runs. Don't be a mile-counter.

(8) Now that you have the tools, work out your own schedule.

(1) (For healthy females 15–40) Same as (1) above.

(2) Drink a lot of hot tea. Do stretching exercises. Sweat. Crap. Think heroic thoughts.

(3) Jog 1 mile, then run as in (6) above except do only 2 miles. Do this three to five days per week. Repeat steps (2) and (3) for five weeks.

(4) Same as (8) above.

Note: For both males and females, don't eat a few hours before running. Assuming your heart is normal, you ought to give it a try. It might save you $547 per year and keep you from the guru's clutches all at the same time.

* Home Remedies *

Around here everyone is a "herbalist," it seems, and is chock full of lore as to what concoction to torture yourself with for any given ailment. Not to be outdone, here's mine—all tried and true:

* Constipation—roughage; moonshine; run 3 miles

* Gas—moonshine

* Menstrual problems—tell the rotten SOB how
rotten he is; moonshine

* Upset stomach—moonshine

* Dental Care *

Daddy entreats me to avoid dentists. His parents diligently sent him and his brother and the result is that the two of them scarce have ten sound teeth between them. Every tooth Daddy ever had filled has given him trouble in later years. Contrariwise, no tooth untouched by a dentist has ever given him any trouble, even though some have cavities of long duration. The only conclusion we can draw is that the remedy is worse than the ailment. By "trouble" I mean excruciating pain and/or the loss of service of a tooth.

Mom spent a small fortune and hours of agony having "root canals" done on her teeth, and they crumbled in just two years. Don't take my word for this but do let me urge you to draw your own conclusions, from your own experiences about dentistry, same as you'd do about the claims made for, say, voodoo.

* Various Therapies *

I've conditioned myself so that when I hear the word "therapy" my check-writing hand automatically clenches shut and stays that way until the danger is past.

I don't intend to set myself up as an expert here, but I do want to urge you again to use your common sense and judge from your experiences rather than be swayed by authority. Keep in mind that the therapist gets his living and his status from being an authority—what's he going to do, go around saying his ideas might be nonsense? He probably didn't realize they were nonsense until after he became an authority, when it was too late to back down from them. You wouldn't really expect him to throw away his whole investment in his career just because it happens to be nonsense, would you?

From my experiences here are a few examples. I offer them as straws in the wind, not as the word straight out of Mt. Sinai.

* When I was a child I didn't speak properly. The school authorities said I needed "speech therapy." I didn't get it, for various reasons, and yet I outgrew the difficulties in another year. And today, why you can scarce tell me from Demosthenes.

* My brother Carl had trouble learning to read and write. The school psychiatrist said he needed special instructions, and to prescribe the nature of the instruction he would have to have Carl tested at an institution. The tests cost us $50. Mom was practically hysterical over the shrink's diagnosis—the dread scourge of dyslexia. Because we moved, Carl never did get "the special instructions he needed." Today he gets B's in reading and writing.

* One of our neighbor's kids was "troubled" and

needed psychiatric assistance (at $50 a whack). After three sessions the family could no longer afford to send him. (The shrink actually called up and tried to wheedle more business out of this working-class family.) Today the kid has outgrown his problems and is as good a citizen as anyone could desire. Why you can scarce tell him from Abraham Lincoln.

* Today orthopedic shoes are often prescribed for babies (so they shouldn't grow up with deformed feet). Now I ask you to use your common sense—how many adults do you know who grew up before the days of orthopedic shoes and have deformed feet? I don't know any, but I do know people who pay $25 a pair for shoes their kid outgrows every four months.

Seeking peace of mind can cost you money, too. Some people get off cheap with church contributions, but nonreligious folks are fair game for an increasing horde of movement hucksters. Interestingly enough, fear of death can be produced clinically—it's a side effect of certain prescription drugs and is a frequent component of delirium tremens. (Remember Huck's Pap wrestling with the Death Angel in *Huckleberry Finn*?) Malnutrition, even in people who think they're well fed, can also be a contributing factor. Solitude—even in a crowd—is another. On the other hand, a nonchalant indifference to the prospect of death, even in individuals not actively unhappy with life, is often observed in untreated diabetics and persons on a high fat-low carbohydrate diet.

In this area, physical health, psychology, and philosophy are mixed together all higgledy-piggledy and you have to sort things out on your own. But don't think you have to buy your way out, because chances are you don't—and can't.

Daddy and I frequently listen to interview programs on the radio, and sometimes some gloomy, solemn person will be on pushing the latest peace-of-mind therapy. We look at each other and laugh because, you see, we're reading each other's mind. "Christ, what *wouldn't* a three-mile run do for this poor bastard?" we're thinking.

The solitude-even-in-a-crowd problem can be quite serious, of course. If you have no one with whom to share your thoughts and feelings, you might as well be in solitary—and solitary has been known to break down even hardened criminals. If you have this problem, recognize its true nature and take steps to solve it. Don't imagine you can get by with substitutes.

As I mentioned in a previous chapter, I'm not in the purpose-of-life business. However, I will say this: I firmly believe that anyone leading a natural, healthy, unharassed life will come to find that life is purposeful and good.

20.
Daily Living

Now that you know how to become a member of the leisure class, you may wonder just what it is we leisure-niks do all day.

Sometimes people will tell us that if they didn't have a job to go to, or a regular routine of duties and responsibilities, they wouldn't know what to do—they'd be bored to death. Boredom is not to be underestimated. Murders, suicides, and even full-scale wars have come about from pure boredom. (Napoleon justified his career on the grounds that he gave men the opportunity to die with military glory rather than of boredom. Women, too, are vulnerable. "Housewife syndrome"—the daily occurrence of eventlessness— is a major problem in our society. In 6th-century Constantinople, Empress Theodora established a convent for reformed prostitutes, so they wouldn't be forced to resume business. Some of the "saved" girls manifested their gratefulness by leaping out of the windows—literally bored to death.) But occasionally being bored is part of life, so don't overestimate it, either. (Nietzsche said, "Against boredom even the gods struggle in vain.")

TV is, of course, the modern way to alleviate boredom, but we don't have one. People are always trying to give us their old TVs, but we decline. We can't handle TV. It absolutely fascinates me when I see it, but I always feel nervous next day when I wake up and realize I've attuned my thoughts to a TV program I've seen—something unreal! My instincts warn me there's a stalking horse in the field. What predator might not be hiding behind the stalking horse of TV? If you can handle TV there's no reason you shouldn't enjoy it—it's just not for us.

We haven't found boredom to be a problem except during the dismal months of the last two winters, which were exceptionally nasty ones. Generally if we are able to get out-of-doors, to exercise properly (run) on a regular basis, eat properly, and be free of outside pressures and harassment, all else falls into place—life is good.

We aren't hermits and neither need you be if you take up this lifestyle. We have friends who invite us to their parties even though they know we aren't in a position to reciprocate (which proves them to be true friends). Friends and neighbors stop by here for a drop of the creature and a hand or two of cards, and we do them the same way. I get the impression some of our friends like to visit here to get a respite from the gracious living they're forced to endure at home. Here they can throw ashes and nutshells on the floor and put their feet up on the table if they want.

I go on dates same as any other girl. If you want to be a hermit or a hippie there's no reason you shouldn't, but you don't have to be one just because you don't happen to have any visible means of support.

* Autumn *

Autumn is busy, but pleasantly so. I guess we average about five hours each of work per day, but living possum-style there is often no clearcut differentiation between one's work, leisure, and recreation. When you're out on a beautiful day gathering nuts for food and bird watching for recreation at the same time, for instance, how much of the time spent is work? It's as anthropologists say about hunting tribes—hunters don't need hobbies, their work is their hobby.

Here's a typical autumn day: If it's nice outside, after breakfast Daddy will cut bunny greens or do garden work, and I'll clean house or dry food. After lunch we'll glean harvested fields, or gather nuts, or go fishing. And since it's migration time, I do a lot of bird watching. Then we might play a little badminton and run. In the evening we'll read or visit.

In bad weather we'll do a lot of food preserving (except drying)—all the last cucumbers, tomatoes, okra, etc. must be pickled before the first frost. And we'll start weatherproofing the house for winter. Of course, this being an anarchy, we might just spend the day reading, studying, hiking, or playing games, if that's our mood.

* Dolly's Autumn Doggerel *

Sun kisses cheek, breeze musses hair,
Geese call to us from high in air.
"Come fly with us!" the leader cries,
Exultant in the autumn skies.
We laugh and wave them on their way,
We'd love to go but can't today.

* Winter *

I will not kid you. Winter is hard to get through for possums. (Their ears freeze and chips break off, leaving them with notched ears.) Since I spent the first eight years of my life in sunny Florida, these northern winters really bug me.

There's only about two hours of actual work (chopping firewood, feeding the creatures, distilling, housework, etc.) each day for each of us, and the rest of the time is something of a battle against boredom. We find we have little interest in preparing the elaborate meals we enjoy in other seasons, and just eat to live.

Having little else to do, and appreciating the money, Daddy will work for a week or two at a time in the winter. A friend of ours contracts for home remodeling and is often able to use an extra hand.

These past two winters the weather was so bad we often had to go a week or more without being able to get out and run. (Daddy once got pneumonia from running in severe weather, so now he doesn't take chances.) Since we seem to have an actual physiological need for strenuous exercise, its lack adds to the general gloom. However, we are able to get something of a workout with our punch-a-rooty. A punch-a-rooty is a small rubber ball tied with a string from a light fixture so as to hang at eye level. It's used as a punching bag.

We read a lot and I pursue my studies. I quit school in seventh grade and now feel this compulsion to be constantly "improving my mind" (if any). How did it happen I quit school in seventh grade? Daddy thinks compulsory education is a fraud—nothing but glorified babysitting—and I hated it, so he simply told the principal we were moving to California, and I never went back. At the time, I thought the principal would find out and send the Gestapo to come at night and take Daddy out back and shoot a bullet through his head, but it never did happen. Mom didn't really approve of this, same as she didn't approve of other of Daddy's ways. She used to say that some day the truant officer, IRS auditors, the game warden, and revenuers would all show up at once.

Not having to go to school, I had time to actually learn something interesting and useful such as how to make moonshine, how to buy a house at a sheriff sale, how to make money in business, how to repair a house, and even how to read and write—these last two being more than you can say for 14.29% of the 1976 high school seniors of the Philadelphia public school system. What would I have learned if I had stayed in school? Exactly what the slowest member of the class would have learned, because that's how they teach. And the subjects! Social studies, forsooth! And new math, where you learn all about "sets" and graduate not knowing how to balance a checkbook. And home economics, where they teach you to be as uneconomical as possible—Betty Crocker propaganda. We take a do-it-yourself approach to education same as any other subject. If we want to learn something, we go to the library, get a book on the subject, and study it. Or we ask questions of someone who really knows the subject, which leaves out most professional teachers.

But back to wintertime at home. Daddy kills the time with mathematics. Math is a pretty good opiate to dull the pain of a Northeast winter. And we play various games. Besides such games as chess and go, we play poetry games and the Alliteration Game. (Awful alliterations are always amusing and accordingly alleviate annually arriving arctic-like atmospheric atrocities.) Watching the birds at the feeding station is a pleasant wintry pastime. Or we practice our music—Daddy has a zither and I have a harmonica. It being winter, and the windows all closed up, the neighbors are spared the atrocities we commit on these instruments.

About the middle of February we start plants indoors for the garden, and plan the garden. It's a real exercise of faith to plot out where the corn, tomatoes, and other vegetables are going to grow when a howling blizzard is in progress over the ground where they are to be planted.

Visiting friends is good, and we do a lot of that, and then, too, they visit us. Then there's BOYS!—but enough of that.

* Spring *

Spring is the busiest time of our year. The garden needs attention—trees and vines need pruning—fish need catching—migrating birds need identifying—it's just one thing after another, it seems. Again, work and recreation can't be separated time-clockwise. Mark Twain's definition of work—"That which you do when you'd rather be doing something else"—hardly fits digging in your garden or going fishing, even if that is how you get your food.

Spring-time to us means asparagus, trout, and a vase of forsythias and pussy willows on the table.

* Summer *

We arise early, while it's still cool, and immediately go outside to see what sort of day God has sent us. As the sun rises higher, my portulacas wake up and I say, "Morning, sweethearts!" to them as they start opening.

Daddy generally gets out the badminton things and we "pitty-pat" a half hour or so. Won't nothing do but I must wear my broad-rimmed straw hat, call him "Reggie," while he calls me "Gwennie," and we use exaggerated British accents while we play. I sometimes wonder how I put up with it.

Then he goes to cut a bucket or two of fodder for the rabbits while I make breakfast and tea. When the bugs aren't bad, we have breakfast on the porch.

After breakfast, I spend several hours Improving My Mind. Daddy, meanwhile, finishes caring for the creatures and generally wanders down to putter around in the garden. He lets out the chickens to keep him company.

Later I'll clean up the house and Daddy takes care of some of the little chores that keep popping up. Since we don't have "convenience foods," lunch takes well over an hour to prepare, so we allow for that. In the summer it's our big meal of the day. Most often it is fried fish, with peas, or corn, or whatever from the garden, wheaten cakes, a huge green salad from the garden, and a bottle of wine or moonshine mint juleps. Sometimes it's rabbit or turtle. We often dine outdoors, under the maple trees or by the garden. After lunch, we're in a pretty jolly mood and fiddle around for an hour or so. We found a little plastic boat and we sometimes take turns paddling around in the lake in it—it holds only one of us at a time.

Then Daddy usually goes off for some fishing, for tomorrow's lunch, and I go bird watching or swimming or finish up the housework. About 3 o'clock we're back and take a nap for two hours or so.

Upon awakening and arguing who's to get up first and make the tea, it's more badminton for a warm-up, and then it's time to run. I always get nervous and scared, and Daddy, the old veteran, always chides me, tells me how it's going to hurt, asks me if I'm a peasant or a member of the Warrior Class, and other pleasant things. "Sissy! Ninny!" he gently encourages me, between humming bars from Wagner's "Entrance of the Gods into Valhalla."

Off we go. The first mile we're together, running easy, for a warm-up. Then the adrenalin starts working. He goes one way, for a 4-mile total, and I go another for a 3-mile total. We both pick up the pace. When he goes the 4-mile route he tries to catch me before I get home, but he can't do it any more. He's getting slower, and I'm getting faster. (I'm on the right side of increasing age and he's on the wrong side.)

After cooling off, I like to go for a swim in the creek, and Daddy cleans fish, cuts bunny greens, and prepares a light supper. Evening is often social time.

Occasionally we decide to go for snapping turtles, and that breaks up the whole routine, since we're up at night and sleeping by day.

* What's Gonna Happen Next? *

It might occur to you that getting off the 9-to-5 treadmill is what you want and need right now but that spending the rest of your life on a half-acre Garden of Eden isn't the whole answer either. Good thinking.

One thing that living possum-style does is to give a person the confidence to have freedom of choice. It's quite likely, for example, that I'll get a job some day: to see what's going on out there in the "real world" and to meet—well, you know—*men*. But I'll never, never get myself into a situation where I *need* a job. If a job annoys me at all—back to possum living here at my Snug Harbor.

This freedom I harp on isn't restricted merely to whether or not to have a job. Now that we have some practice at it, I'm pretty sure we can possum live *anywhere*. And that means we can travel. I have an idea in the back of my head to build a flat-bottomed boat small enough to be rowed or poled but big enough to afford sleeping room for two under a canvas shelter. We would then take off down the intercoastal waterway from Philadelphia to my birthplace in Florida, and return. The whole trip would take about a year, and we'd live off the land (and water) the whole time. What an adventure! We'd rent out the house for the year, which should more than pay for the boat and expenses. (Now all I have to do is to talk Daddy—or someone else—into coming along to help do the rowing and poling.)

So that's how the last four years have drifted by for us.

Now, then, don't you have a hobby you just don't have time to pursue? Golf? Tennis? Partying? Studying? Music? Painting? Pottery? Hang gliding? Whatever? Even fishing or gardening— wouldn't you like to change these from merely recreation to partly occupation?

Yes? Then why don't you simply do so?

It's feasible. It's easy. It *can* be done. It *should* be done.

Do it.

Afterword

Possum Living: Tried and True Lessons

I wrote *Possum Living* more than 30 years ago when I was a cocky 18-year-old. The amazing thing is how it's still right on target. Prices and technology have changed, but the principles are the same.

Self-reliance gives one a strong sense of security.

There's a great feeling of reassurance in knowing that if the chips were down, you could live on very, very little money. I'm not sure how my family would adjust to living on ground wheat and rabbits and, living in coastal Texas, I'd sure hate to give up air-conditioning, but I know if we had to, we'd be fine. Just knowing how to possum live takes away a great deal of the fear brought on by the fluctuating economy, Y2K-type scares, and unstable job markets.

One needs very few physical things in order to be happy.

The physical things needed to be happy? Water, food, shelter, good health, security, and liberty—that's it. Everything else is mental. Material things for the sake of material things will not make you happy. Anything more than the basic six is just icing on the cake: nice, but not necessary.

Being happy, even, may not be the end goal of a worthwhile life. Often being engaged and interested is just as satisfying. Many important tasks are hard and you aren't happy while you're doing them, but you are engaged and involved and that can be just as good, sometimes better.

Many other people have also thought this. Viktor Frankl wrote about it in *Man's Search for Meaning*. When my father and I were possum living, we brought meaning to our lives through learning and by being good friends and neighbors. Eventually, I wanted to do more and be part of the bigger picture—that's why I wrote *Possum Living* and why I eventually moved on from it.

When I was younger, my goal was to make a difference in the world. Now that I am older, I can't run or do vigorous exercise because of joint problems (a genetic gift from my mom's side of the family) and I can't handle stress like I used to. So my goal right now is to have a serene life. I find myself turning inward to my home, my family, and my community. And once again, not wanting things frees me to take the path I need to take.

Look carefully at life and your choices.

Sometimes in life we are too busy to do more than survive. When you have little children or sick parents or a major illness, you may not have any choice other than to just keep soldiering on. But if you wake up in the middle of the night and think, "What in the world am I doing with my life?" then you need to listen to that little voice.

The whole point of *Possum Living* is that you have choices; you can take control of your life. If you are reading this and you live in a highly developed society such as the United States, you have choices undreamed of by even the greatest emperors of the past. You can be rich, you can be educated, you can be lazy, you can help the world. You have choices, but to exercise those choices you need a bit of economic freedom. Set your mind to a few years of really hard work and scrimping. Give yourself a doable time line, say, three years. If you need inspiration, watch the documentary *God Grew Tired of Us* to see what hard work and scrimping can accomplish in a few years. When it comes to spending, tell yourself, "Not now, maybe later." Even if you don't decide to go the whole possum, a little economic freedom will go a long way in giving you choices.

Dad taught me to look carefully not just at my life and my choices, but at society's, too. Living with Dad was like living with an anthropologist studying a foreign culture. Why do people do this? Why does society have that convention? He looked at things. He questioned them. And it made me realize that the majority of what goes on is done by convention. Every society needs rules to function. To get along harmoniously, you don't want people lying, cheating, and stealing. But many of the rules are arbitrary.

Before I decide that a rule or convention isn't important, I try to figure out why it was made in the first place. This is an interesting mental exercise that gives you a great deal of insight into your own culture. My dad, I'm afraid, would often just dismiss rules out of hand. Under his influence, I advocated some activities in the "Law" chapter that I now consider wrong.

During our time possum living in semirural Pennsylvania we lived near a large reservoir that had a perimeter of preserved land to keep the water clean. Surrounding this band of wildness were acres and acres of rolling farmland, hedgerows, and wooded streams. Well, the inevitable happened and developers started to buy up the land. We were heartbroken to see such beautiful land put under concrete and Dad decided to take matters into his own hands. One night, he went to the houses that were being built, cut the electrical wires, and burned down the houses. The next week, the builders started rebuilding the exact same houses. Dad burned them down again. This happened three times before he gave up. And for all his efforts, the only result was an article in the local paper complaining about the vandalism. The people who were effective in doing something were the ones who banded together and pushed for a large park to protect the most valuable wildlife areas and for zoning to prevent houses from being built too densely around the lake.

A year later, I was taking a free first-aid class at the local library when I got to talking to a young lady who, just a few months earlier, had moved near the lake. She told me that although she loved the area, she had been afraid to move into the new house because someone kept burning it down. That's when I learned that these things always involve real people with real feelings. I think my "rebellion" as an older teen was to become law-abiding (mostly).

When Dad died, I spread his ashes on the land he loved so much.

Do your research.

I learned this in my possum days, but I have to keep relearning it. For instance, when I moved to coastal Texas, I blithely set up a garden *without researching local gardening methods*. Using the double-trenching method on our flat gumbo clay was a recipe for disaster. After a wet summer wiped out my entire garden, I looked up the local organic gardening group and, lo and behold, they had a guide on the best gardening techniques, varieties, and planting times for this area. Man, I could have saved myself a lot of trouble if I had done my research first!

If you are researching how to possum live, this book is a great start, but update your research, too. Hell, I have no idea how much of the info I wrote on buying a house in foreclosure is still correct. And if you want to hunt, fish, and forage, the Internet can be your best buddy. (Your local library probably gives free access.) Look up invasive species—you'll be doing everyone a favor if you eat them.

Small steps lead to big goals.

When we were possums and needed something done, Dad would say, "Hell, we can do that!" We would talk to people who knew how to do it or research it in the library. Then we would figure out what we needed and buy, scrounge, or make the supplies. When we had everything lined up, we jumped right in, and adjusted as we went along. It gave me an "I can do that" attitude that has carried me far. Just break a goal into smaller steps. Figure out the first step and take it. Then figure out the second step and take it. Each step closer to your goal will make the next step clearer. Even missteps are better than no steps. This is simple and obvious but powerful.

When I wanted to write a book, I wrote it out in pencil. Then I got a typewriter and taught myself to type. Next, I went to the library and looked up publishers. None took me on, but one suggested getting an agent. I went back to the library and got a list of agents. One agent took *Possum Living* on and sold it to a small publisher. That publishing house sold it to a big publisher and the rest is history. Before I knew it, I went from being a hick with a GED and no typing skills to a published author on a publicity tour (which even included a national TV appearance on *The Merv Griffin Show*).

The same process helped me to become a NASA aerospace engineer. I couldn't afford to go to college, so I worked hard and saved money. Not having a high school transcript, I knew my acceptance to college was going to be based on my SAT scores. I bought a study book and for one month all I did was study for the SATs. With good scores in hand, I was accepted to several universities, but couldn't afford most of them. (It never occurred to me to ask for a scholarship. Dad had beaten it into my head that it was not honorable to take money you hadn't earned or weren't going to repay. I'm not so stuck on that now. Feel free to send me money anytime.) During my first two years, all I took were liberal arts classes at inexpensive schools. I knew I wanted to work at NASA, so I called their personnel office and learned that they were only hiring co-ops. (Co-ops are students who work in their field for a while to earn college credits.) In my third year, I transferred to a private school with a co-op program. The school didn't have an agreement with the NASA site where I wanted to work, Langley, so I called Langley's co-op office and got them to agree to open a contract at my school. Sure enough, I became a co-op and was eventually hired by NASA full-time. While at Langley, I met my future husband. (Of course, it wasn't too hard to catch his eye—I was the only girl in my branch.) He's the best part of my engineering career!

When I wanted to change careers to be an environmental educator, I took a job as a receptionist at the local nature center to be sure I really wanted to work in that field. None of the local universities offered an environmental education degree, so I got a master's in science education with a specialization in biology. When I graduated, the Houston economy was going through a downturn and people were complaining about the lack of jobs in my field. I went to every park and nature center in the area and started talking with people who worked there. Eventually, I came across a manager who wanted to start an environmental education program but had very little money or resources to do so. Well, wasn't I the expert on doing things without much money or resources? I offered to set up a program for her over the summer on a trial basis. It was a success and she convinced her boss to hire me as an administrative assistant and paid me way more than I would have ever asked for.

Small steps to a big goal. It really works.

Little amounts of time and money add up.

Being miserly taught me how little amounts of money add up. Wanting to do a lot in life taught me how little amounts of time add up. Getting rid of extraneous things not only saves money, it also saves time, and time is the one thing you can never make more of.

I stopped wearing makeup when I realized that it took at least 15 minutes a day to apply. I estimate that over the last 30 years, I've saved 163,800 minutes of my life for other things by not wearing makeup (15 minutes a day x 7 days a week x 52 weeks a year x 30 years or what amounts to 114 days of nonstop makeup applying). Not to mention saving thousands and thousands of dollars—probably more than $12,000 in 2009 dollars. It didn't seem to hurt my prospects with the boys, either.

Even my kids have picked up on the idea that little bits add up to big amounts. My daughter, Maria, has wanted to travel ever since she was little. She saved up her whopping $5/month allowance, pet-sitting money, birthday money, etc., until, at the age of 12, she had enough money to pay for a 10-day trip to China.

That same year, my 17-year-old son demonstrated that he had a grasp of the concept, if not the details. We had repeatedly told David that we were not paying for his college education. We went to college on our own and he could do it on his own. This annoyed him to no end because all of his friends' parents were going to help them. We told him that his friends' parents probably loved them more than we love him, but he didn't buy it. So we told him we just didn't have enough money and I wasn't going to work full-time to pay for his college, that it would be too stressful and not fair to the rest of the family. He replied that we would have the extra money if we didn't live such a luxurious lifestyle.

I said, "David, do you mean the fact that we live in a nice house in a nice neighborhood?"

"No, the house and the neighborhood are about right."

"Do you mean the trip that Maria and I are planning to China?"

"No, Maria has saved up for her trip and I think you're going through a midlife crisis."

"Do you mean that I spend too much on groceries?"

"No, I like all the good food you make,"

"David, please tell me how we are spending too much money on luxuries because it's escaping me right now."

He thought for a minute and said, "We have way too many refrigerator magnets."

Be wary of the shoulds.

Well, not all the shoulds; you should be a good person, you should be responsible, you should support yourself and your children, and you should be a good neighbor. But after that, look at them very closely.

My husband grew up in a tight-fisted family and yet sometimes he will say, "I work hard, I *should* be able to have . . ." and he will look like a dejected puppy or count himself a failure. He'll bemoan the fact that we are "poor." And then I have to remind him that we aren't poor; we're frugal. We value free time and control of our choices over spending money.

Even I'll get hit sometimes with the notion that I *should* have something. To get over the idea, I tell myself, "Not now, maybe later." Then I'll think about the resources used to make and transport the item, how much of my time it will take to get it and to take care of it; I'll calculate how many hours I'd have to work to pay for it, and what will happen to it when I throw it away.

I visualize my own personal landfill in the backyard. There are not too many material desires that can withstand an onslaught like that!

There are also questionable shoulds about what we do in life. After I had been at NASA for a while, I realized that I had worked very hard to get a job that wasn't right for me. I needed to be outside more, I needed more variety and flexibility, and I needed more time in nature. I kept telling myself, I *should* be a NASA engineer—I had invested a lot of time, money, and effort in becoming one, it was important, and I was good at it. I *should* be happy—but I wasn't. At this point my husband was the one who told me to forget the shoulds. He encouraged me to take a sabbatical, told me that I hadn't been a fool choosing to become an engineer because, hey, I met him, and suggested that, since we had saved up a bunch of money, this was a good time to start a family.

Meanwhile, I was volunteering at the local nature center. A clue to the right work for you is what you will do for free. Studying nature and teaching about it *hummed* for me. As Joseph Campbell advised, follow your bliss: "If you do follow your bliss you put yourself on a kind of track that has been there all the while, waiting for you, and the life that you ought to be living is the one you are living."

TV is a stalking horse.

Television is like a loud salesman in your living room.

Sometimes he's interesting, frequently he's embarrassing, and always he's trying to sell you stuff.

The whole purpose of mainstream TV is to get you to buy things—not to entertain you or teach you or make you feel you belong, but to get you to spend money. Think about it: millions and millions of dollars and thousands and thousands of hours of man power put in by clever people just to get you, personally, to buy stuff. They will resort to almost anything to accomplish this. They will make you feel you are inadequate, a failure, a bad parent, incomplete; they will use any method and pander to your basest instincts to get you to spend money. Just like most of the people on TV are better looking than you, most of the homes, cars, and possessions are better than yours. This will affect you even if you swear it doesn't. And if they can't get you with ads, hypermaterialism, or product placement, they will promote shows that breed envy and discontent, such as "Lifestyles of the Beautiful and Ostentatious" or "Exorbitant Fabulous Houses." They will even try to sell you leisure time so you can have a break from your hectic lifestyle of earning money to buy things.

You can get the benefits of television programming without all the pressure if you just disconnect the TV and use the library or Netflix to get DVDs. If you combine this with a little Internet research, you can completely control the content of what enters your home in the guise of entertainment.

Never forget that the whole purpose of TV is to make you want to spend money. Of course, newspapers, magazines, and the Internet present the same problem, but it's a lot easier to ignore the obvious advertising and rampant commercialism posing as stories in written media.

Hold on to the good, let go of the bad.

You don't always have control over good or bad things happening in your life. Sometimes the best you can do is to hold on to the good and let go of the bad. I learned this lesson the hardest with my dad.

What happened to my dad? Dad was a true genetic alcoholic. His own father was and his mother's mother was. He got it from both sides of the family. Of all the things I am thankful for in my life, I am most thankful that I was not born an alcoholic. When my dad's drinking was under control, he was charming, clever, and loving. When it wasn't, he was needy, nasty, and paranoid. During most of the time that I lived with my dad after my parents divorced, he was a wonderful person. But toward the end, alcoholism twisted and crushed him. It drove away everyone who loved him. For many years after I left home, I tried to stay close, but he became desperate and violent over time. He threatened me, my boyfriends, my brother, my brother's wife, my mother, my friends; he even threatened to hurt himself. We tried hard to get him help and thought of having him committed, but he adamantly refused to accept help. He completely denied he was an alcoholic. When he pulled a gun on my brother's family and threatened my fiancé, I decided I had to cut all ties. I never communicated with him again. It was very, very hard. It was the hardest thing I've ever done—so hard that I ended up seeing a psychologist to deal with the pain. Many years later when I learned that he had died in a car accident, I cried for him and I cried for me, but mainly, I cried for what might have been.

And yet, who I am and who my children are is a part of who he was. The thing that Dad taught me, on the most profound level, is that you have *choices* in life. Deep choices. And for that, he has my undying gratitude.

You will change your opinion on a few things over the years.

You never saw backpedaling like I did when my smug 14-year-old daughter read to me the part in *Possum Living* about having kids without getting married. Some fun! But really, if you are going to have kids, you want the commitment and strength you can get from a spouse. Trust me, I know.

And I completely repudiate what I said under "Law." I have learned that life is more pleasant and your actions are more effective when you are polite but firm. Call the cops if you need to, band together to get action, challenge authority, but be polite. Firmness works, intimidation doesn't (at least not in the long run). This is true for causes, relationships, and childrearing.

Sometimes the turtles get revenge.

For several years, I taught field biology to gifted-and-talented (aka "smart") fifth graders who were bused to a local university for special classes. Once, while doing population sampling (aka "fishing") at a pond on campus, one student accidentally hooked a big turtle on his line. Not wanting to have the student get bit or the turtle get hurt, I told him to gently pull the line in and I would free the turtle. I lay down on the bank, reached over the edge, and grabbed the turtle by the shell.

Suddenly, I started sliding down the damp, grassy slope. Realizing that my students would never let me live it down if I slid headfirst into the pond, I instinctively jerked back and up. This put the turtle at the exact level of my soft, white neck and it clamped down as hard as it could. It hurt like hell! There I was with a 5-pound turtle hanging from my neck, all the kids staring at me openmouthed, and I couldn't get the turtle off! Ignoring the pain, I pulled and pulled but it wouldn't come off! I had visions of walking up to the university building and wandering around with a large turtle hanging from my neck and a line of kids following me through the halls until I could find someone with a screwdriver to pry the damn thing off. Desperately, I tugged with all my strength and it finally came off, leaving me with an enormous hickey and endless teasing from my students.

A FINAL BIT OF WISDOM

I aim to be a good person because it makes me happy; it makes people around me happy; it makes society work better; and it helps to create the type of society in which I want to live. I am going to die anyway and I want to have lived with honor, grace, happiness, and kind deeds.

Ask yourself what you aim to be and what you should be doing. Are you living the life you ought to be living? If yes, then good luck to you. If not, then start taking control of your life.

It *can* be done. It *should* be done.

Do it.

You don't have forever.

About the Author

Following her success as an author, Dolly Freed grew up to be a NASA aerospace engineer. That is, after acing the SATs with an education she received from the public library and putting herself through college. She's also been an environmental educator, business owner, and college professor. She lives in Texas with her husband and two children.